THE OFFENDER I ONCE DEFENDED

D.A. GOODWIN

Copyright © 2016 by D.A. Goodwin
Cover design by New Direction Group
Cover images by Walter Priece Photography

All rights reserved. This book or any portion thereof may not be reproduced or used in any manner whatsoever without the express written permission of the publisher.

First printing: 2016
ISBN: 978-1-329-88662-9
Edited by Your Editing Pro (YEP): www.youreditingpro.net

Some names and places have been changed in the writing of this memoir.

FOR MY FAMILY, WITH LOVE

THE OFFENDER I ONCE DEFENDED

1

My Apologies

I've been paralyzed before. With fear. Fear that masked men would burst into our backdoor at night and try to rape me. Fear that I would have to protect my boys and husband by running for the gun, grabbing it, scrambling to focus it in the dark, and squeezing the trigger.

But going through all of that to only discover that I didn't know how to turn the gun off of safety mode....

I've been paralyzed with other fears too. Fear that a weird creep would follow me home from work. Fear that my husband would be followed, attacked, or killed because of his banking job. Fear that our children would be deceived with kind words and then kidnapped.

When those fears plagued my dreams, I was awakened into the reality that with the exception of my eyes and pounding heart, my body was completely paralyzed. I'd found myself on my back frozen, yet sweating, with my eyes wide open, carefully watching the hallway shadows outside of my bedroom door. And I still couldn't move.

Every time it happened, calling on Jesus was the only way I was released from my paralysis, released from my nightmare.

The nightmares were actually new for me. That's because fearing no person and no thing had been ingrained in me throughout my entire childhood. It eventually carried me through the majority of my adulthood.

That was until a few years ago...

You see, when you grow up in what's been later deemed by the FBI as being the most dangerous city in the whole state, of course, you learn a few things about protecting yourself when you're in potentially dangerous situations. Now when you become an adult, the way you decide to handle those potentially dangerous situations is on you.

***

I was raised the right way. My mama taught us to choose to do the right thing over the wrong thing and to only fight back if someone hit us first. There probably wasn't a child raised in Dillon County who was not taught how to physically fight.

I had older siblings and a slew of fighting cousins to teach me. When you were young, you even played fighting, meaning you and your partner (usually my big brother) balled up your fists and swung punches at each other until one person conquered the other and made him or her have to step way back to avoid the incoming swings. It prepared you so you'd know how to protect yourself if you ever got into a real fight.

You only messed up when one partner mistakenly hit the other too hard. Now those were the worst fights! And for that reason, my mama didn't allow us to "play fight." We just snuck and did it when she was at work. We knew we'd never get caught unless we got into a real fight. And if we did, that's when we got into trouble. We didn't want that, so we were really careful when we did play like that.

Even as a child, I didn't get into many fights or much trouble at all. That was with the exception of the day that the fifth grade bus monitor offended me. I know I'll probably be regretting that day for the rest of my life.

***

Every afternoon when the last bell rang signaling school was out, the bus riders at Gordon Elementary had to line up on both sides of the long hallways to wait on the buses to arrive. And every afternoon we were under the watchful eyes of a selected "hall monitor."

One Friday afternoon, a quiet fifth grader named Danny had been chosen to be the monitor on our end of the hall. Danny also rode Bus 13 with us and never said too much to us fourth graders, so I was quite surprised and a bit embarrassed when she told me to turn around into the fire drill position for talking.

There was absolutely no way that she could've heard me talking to my cousin Paige. Of course, I was talking, which I didn't admit to then, but there was no way that Danny could have actually heard me. Not from where she was standing.

Besides, my teeth were clenched together into a wide smile, and I was talking through those clenched teeth. When I had to turn around, knowing that she couldn't hear me speaking, I was pretty pissed.

Yet, I did as I was told. Partially, anyway.

Rolling my eyes, I methodically stooped my knees to the uncomfortable concrete floor and turned around to face the wall. I lowered my head for just a second but only to raise it again, look at Danny, and wait for her to catch my eyes.

"I'M GONNA GET YOU WHEN WE GET OUTSIDE..." I slowly mouthed the words, guaranteeing that she read my lips correctly before I lowered my head and turned back around into the fire drill position.

I don't know what the heck I was thinking at the time. Apparently, nothing good, especially not with what I did next.

When Bus 13 was called, it was always a rush to get to it, although I doubt our bus driver would purposefully leave any of us for walking slowly. Still, we swiftly walked to the bus.

That was until I felt someone stepping on my heels.

I whipped my head to the right and low and behold, there was Danny.

I lost it.

I pounced on her as if I had been waiting to do it for years. And I immediately regretted it. She didn't deserve it, even if she hadn't heard me talking, she knew I was and had called me on it. I was so wrong, and I didn't want God to get me for what I'd done.

If I'd never called on Jesus before, I know I did that day. I could not get suspended. I couldn't miss school and have my grades drop. Then Mommy would have to call somebody to get me from school while she worked out of town. She would surely beat my butt and ground me for that.

I started praying hard asking for forgiveness. Thankfully, it was Friday, and the principal was off. Although the teacher who'd caught us fighting had warned to advise the principal when he arrived on Monday, God spared me, and I never heard back on that discipline. But weeks later, Danny moved away.

I am sincerely sorry, Danny.

***

My childhood made me look at fighting differently as an adult. Because of where I was from and the way I was raised, I had to always be ready to defend myself against anyone and to never show fear, even when I am fearful.

That could be good and bad at the same time. Being a silent fighter with a tamed temper meant that once it flares you have to realize that some people are just not worth going to jail or hell over.

I'm sure some who have heard about the violence in Dillon probably feared going near the small town where black folks often shot at and killed each other during even the broadest of daylights, especially if they were in one of the hoods like Riverdale or Newtown. I've always had relatives that lived in both, but even as an adult I still avoid those areas.

Through the years of my adulthood, I've learned to wait for the reactions and facial expressions of people after telling them the name of the city where I was born and raised. It has never failed. Usually, eyes get bigger, mouths widen a little, and smiles seem to fade from surprise.

In response, I just smile. I've come to realize that when people know where I'm from, some seem to have a little more respect.

2
A Surprise in the Box

Receiving news at the beginning of 2013 that over 500 of us workers would be laid off in ninety days did not come as a shock to me. I can't say the same for those who were wailing with tears and visibly losing their composure.

We were working at one of the largest home mortgage companies in the state doing loan modifications. We, or at least I, figured that the housing crisis was pretty much over when we'd eventually found ourselves scrambling each day to find mortgage modifications to even work on.

So on June 3 when my stilettos did their final pats across that steamy office parking lot, I tossed my sunglasses on and headed to my car. You would've thought I was headed on vacation the way I nonchalantly pranced out of there. Heck, I even used vacation hours to leave a day early. There was no point in sitting there pretending to be doing work that did not exist.

I was ready for a change into a field far away from anything related to money.

And the timing was actually perfect. I had already been accepted into SNHU's online master's program, my husband Kevin was excited to finally have a housewife, and our two sons were out of school for the summer. Being out for the summer also meant there would not be any expensive afterschool bills each week.

In my eyes, money wouldn't be much of an issue since Kevin was still working full-time, and I'd begin receiving unemployment checks within a couple of weeks...not to mention the 401k, retirement money, and severance package I'd be receiving. And there would be no gas money needed to get back and forth across town all day.

I'd even reached out to a local shelter to begin doing volunteer work the very next week. I really felt that life was about to be fulfilling, as I would be able to enjoy the comforts of my cozy home more than ever before.

Days after being laid off, I began volunteering at the transitional house for female victims of domestic violence. It was a relief to find that the director didn't mind if I took Lil' Kevin and Bryant there with me since they were out on summer break. Besides, other children lived at the facility with their moms, so they could play together while I did a bit of work.

Soon, the boys and I were beginning to have a daily routine. We'd get up and get dressed. I'd do schoolwork, and if I needed to run an errand or run to the facility for a brief assignment we'd leave around 11 a.m. and be back at home before 1 p.m.

***

On one day in particular after finishing at the facility, I pulled up to my mailbox and opened the huge metal door. I gasped at what I saw lying on top of the mail that would've just been delivered a few hours earlier.

Was it a joke?

At first, I didn't know whether to laugh or get mad because apparently someone left it there for Kevin or me. But if it were a joke, I sure didn't find it to be laugh-worthy.

The thong-like panties staring back at me were gray and black and looked worn out and dingy. It was as if they'd literally been worn by some young woman every day for the past decade. I looked up at my rearview mirror to see if anyone was walking on the road behind the car.

No one.

Ahead of me: no one.

One last time, I looked up and down the street to see if any young boys were hanging out or looking suspicious, although I already knew there weren't any I'd seen who did that anymore. I assumed that the last group of boys who had walked up and down the neighborhood streets had moved away the other year when we stopped seeing them.

That only left the teenage boy whose relative lived across the street from us in a white, stone house and the two brothers who lived down the dirt road to our right with their family.

The Huck brothers were two chocolate-colored, baby-faced boys who had been in trouble a few times before but seemed to be harmless. In fact, I found them to be quite respectful young men, with the exception of the occasional times they or some of their friends had dropped liquor bottles in our yard late at night probably before stumbling down the dirt road to their house.

Because the Huck brothers were so cute, they shouldn't have had the time to be bothering with Kevin and me, especially when they could have been living fun, single lives and minding their own business.

Both boys were in their twenties and neither had children, which was almost unheard of in the small town I'd grown up in. Heck, some young guys from Dillon had several kids and several baby mamas by the time they hit their twenties. The Hucks weren't that much younger than Kevin and me. They even called us "Mr.

Kevin" and "Mrs. Dawn." How adorable was that? It just couldn't have been either of them who put the panties in my mailbox.

Or could it?

Thinking back on that day, the burgundy Honda with the brothers in it did turn onto the road as I was leaving off of it. But if it was one of them, whose underwear had they stolen that fast? One of their sister's?

First, I doubt they would've made it into the girls' room of their home, let alone made it out with a pair of panties to even put into our mailbox. It really didn't make much sense.

Or could it have been the guy who always walked around the neighborhood asking for food or a ride? I hadn't seen him yet that day. Usually, he walked up and down our street or stood at the stop sign at the end of our road or the one around the block that was close to the Dollar General that he often hung out at.

He was such a pest, the type of person you can't make eye contact with out of fear that he will ask for something or give you a gross physical examination in return. Still, the neighbors like Melissa and Jerry always said that he was harmless.

Could I truly say that he was harmless?

**

I remember the first time I'd seen the guy. It was during the raw, dry heat of the summer in the middle of the day. And there he was, walking by with long sleeves on. Something *had* to have been wrong with him.

The last time I'd seen a grown man walking around with dark, long-sleeved clothing on during a blazing South Carolina day had been when I lived in Dillon and Mr. Dave walked by.

My siblings and I were all quite terrified of Mr. Dave. He had to be at least six feet tall, or so it seemed from a young child's point of view. He always wore a dark blue and black plaid jacket, dark pants, a weird-looking, dark hat, and midnight black shades that didn't allow you to see how his eyes really looked.

To top it off, he was a very dark-skinned, very slender man who was always carrying a bag and a stick with him when he walked by. Whenever we saw him, regardless of what we were doing, our little bodies kind of froze in place, but our big eyes followed him all the way up the road until he was inside his dark, heavily shaded house.

The neighborhood nuisance wasn't tall like Mr. Dave, so I hadn't considered him to be scary at all. That is, with the exception of the time that I heard loud banging on the back door in the middle of the night a couple of years after we'd moved in.

At the time, Kevin was working a second job as a night auditor at a hotel but during the third shift on weekends. I often found myself trying to stay awake until he knocked off of work at seven each morning. That rarely happened. I always seemed to fall asleep on the couch while struggling to watch TV until he arrived.

That night the sound of heavy thuds against the door rattled me from my peaceful dreams. My heart began to bang as if it were trying to escape from my walls. I began to tremor uncontrollably as I stammered from the chair and looked at the digital clock on the cable box.

It was 1:33 in the morning.

It took a second for me to gather myself as the banging continued. I turned toward the front door until realizing that the knock was coming from the back of the house.

The only people who knocked on our backdoor were family members, close friends, or neighbors.

But who could it be at this time of night?

The only time someone else came to a black neighborhood and knocked on a door at night was when a side chick was dropping by for a late night snack, when a weedhead was looking to buy, when a crackhead was feening for a hit, or when a police officer was about to make a drug bust or deliver bad news.

I had no reason to see a side chick and would even dare one to prance on my property. Then, I didn't know of nor care to listen to rumors about any weedheads or crackheads being in the neighborhood. Police officers definitely wouldn't be banging on our back door.

For those reasons, I knew exactly what I had to do.

-13-

If someone with no business being at my house was at my door, I was going to make sure they knew not to come back again.

On my tiptoes, I sprinted to our bedroom and reached my arm to the top of the armoire to feel for the small gun that we kept up high, out of sight and out of our sons' reach. When I felt the Beretta, I grabbed it by the handle and ran to the backdoor. I didn't want the person knocking to leave thinking that no one was home.

Standing by the door with the gun pointed toward the floor and away from my foot, I attempted to look out the foggy peephole. The porch light was already on, as I always kept it lit all night when Kevin was working. Unfortunately, it still wasn't quite bright enough for me to make out the figure. I could only see the shape of a thin man.

"Who is it?" Hearing my shaky voice caught me off guard. *Why was I nervous?*

"It's Scott," answered a man—a man who sounded just like a black man.

I didn't know a black man named Scott who sounded like a black man. The guys named Scott who I'd known were white.

"It's who?"

"Scott! Can I get a ride home? I live back there around the corner, and I smell smoke coming from my house!"

Really? The nerve of him.

I knew that disgusting voice.

And I could not have possibly sounded that gullible in the only five words I'd even spoken. Yet, my hand was violently trembling as I held the deathly grip on the Beretta.

"Hey, get the hell away from my house and don't come in my yard again!" There. I'd found my authoritative voice. "And if you need some help, go to a *man's* house at night and ask for it!" My voice was still a bit shaky, but I hoped the pervert hadn't noticed.

"HAHAHAHA!" The weirdo burst into an ear-piercing laughing spell as if I'd said something funny.

I could not believe that this devil was getting a kick out of trying to terrify me. He had to have seen Kevin leave the house earlier that night. He had to have known that I would be up alone while our young children were asleep. He had to have been watching the house...and me.

Still looking out the peephole, I could see the dark outline turning away from the door and heading down the steps, supposedly leaving the yard. I sprinted over to the kitchen window to watch him leave.

The dark, nameless figure could not be seen anywhere in the pitch black, but a demonic, Chucky-like laughter was echoing through the night, trailing behind him as he strutted further and further away from my yard.

When I called Kevin and told him what happened, less than ten minutes later I was startled, yet again, by another sound at the backdoor. This time, my frozen body sat stiffly on the couch. Paralyzed, I could not move at all.

Suddenly, the voice from the ADT alarm announced, "Back Door," and a concerned Kevin came rushing around the corner towards me.

He had left his night auditor job unattended and was there to check on me! I almost jumped into his arms and bear-hugged him harder than ever. He had already searched the neighborhood looking for the guy.

Thank God, he didn't find him...

The next day, I only heard about the story of Kevin confronting the pest as he nonchalantly attempted to prance by our road as if nothing had happened the night before.

3
He Never Looked Away

Although I had been terrified that night, it wasn't the way I was raised to be. Mommy taught her children to fear no man. She even made us memorize Psalm 23 so that if we were ever afraid we could be reassured that we were protected and comforted by God's weapons: a rod and a staff.

That verse was my comfort as a child, but as an adult with my own family, the Beretta and baseball bats served as wonderful backup.

When we'd first moved to McNair Road, anytime Kevin and I sat on the porch talking and watching the traffic go by while the boys played ball in the yard before us, we usually saw the long-sleeved man slowly walking by.

Sometimes, he'd even yell out, "How you, Sir?" to Kevin.

He was fairly polite, just like all the other neighbors we encountered. I didn't know where he stayed on the block, but I figured it had to be somewhere nearby since we did see him quite often.

The man had been by our house before, coming around to our backdoor to ask for "anything to eat." We never caught the guy's name, but since we recognized him from the neighborhood we didn't hesitate to throw a sandwich together for him while we made him wait outside. We recognized him, but it still didn't mean we knew him.

Not like that.

The first time I caught the nasty man openly watching me was probably towards the end of summer, 2010. At the time, we still didn't know his name. On that day in particular, Kevin, the boys, and I were out in the backyard moving tree limbs as Kevin cut some of the smaller branches from the little forest behind our house. Each time Kevin dropped a branch, the boys and I took turns grabbing them and throwing them onto the back of his burgundy Mazda pickup.

During my last walk to the truck, I suddenly began to feel a bit uncomfortable within my own body as if I were standing in the open yard naked. Eyes seemed to be searching all over me—eyes coming from the direction of the dirt road.

I turned my head towards the beginning of the road, and there he was. The neighborhood pest was standing there, heavily clothed in the steaming heat, his eyes fixed on my every move, and his hands on his hips as if he was worn out from a long day of tiresome work. Pretty much as if he'd been moving tree limbs alongside of us.

When he saw me watching him watching me, I waited for him to look away like most normal people do when they realize the person they're watching has caught onto their stalking eyes.

But he never did look away. Instead, with his disgusting eyes fixated on mine, he slowly inched his dirty, raggedy old shirt up a bit, revealing his boney rib cage that I had not been prepared to see.

"Ew!" I was utterly disgusted at how the pervert had the nerve to stand there and watch me.

He was mighty brave to openly watch any woman whose man was right there with her. Apparently, he didn't care. I looked back to see if Kevin had seen him, but he was busy tousling with a stubborn limb from the thick pine tree. I whipped my head back towards the dirt road, but the man was gone.

Was I seeing ghosts?

Apparently, I wasn't because a moment later, the disgusting man was also in our backyard asking my husband if he could help out for a few dollars. The look I almost snapped my neck to give Kevin quickly answered that question.

After Kevin told the guy "No" and sent him on his way, I asked if he'd seen him standing there watching me. Of course he hadn't, but he did, at least, believe me. And I told Kevin he'd better not ever let the guy help him do any working or lurking at our house.

***

If a man had put panties in our mailbox, what would his reason for it have been? Unless he was doing it to make it look like Kevin was cheating on me with a jealous female who wanted her presence in his life to be known. But what man would go that far to set Kevin up to get next to me?

I couldn't think of any.

I slammed the mailbox door shut, leaving the dirty panties right there. I pulled the car onto the rocky dirt road beside our house that led to the house the Hucks lived in before backing up into the road to turn around and use our first driveway, which led to a gravel path that went all the way around the house and up to our back door.

I did this every day just to avoid hearing Kevin's mouth. He hated when I used the second driveway. He was almost like a detective watching for my car tracks across his freshly cut front lawn. It was so funny that he really thought a few lines would "kill his grass."

I clicked my left signal light on as usual and threw up my hand to speak to my moped-driving neighbor Jerome and another guy, probably a cousin, who were at the back corner of his yard. Jerome was always out there hanging around, usually with a group of guys, or simply working on something. Just what that something was, I didn't know, and didn't pay much attention either.

Jerome and his guests always threw their hands up to speak and minded their business, and we minded ours too. Any other time I saw him was when he was tooting by on that red and black moped. I'll never forget the day when I saw that he had a thick woman on the back towering over him and holding on tightly to his sides.

Now that was a sight to see.

***

I didn't tell my nosey boys what was going on, although Lil' Kevin did, of course, ask why I didn't take the mail that he could clearly see from his spot on the passenger side of the car. I told him because somebody put something nasty in there to be funny, and I was gonna get Dad to get it. Thankfully, our bright youngster let it go before asking a billion questions, as usual.

But who did it?

Could it have been a female my husband had been seeing while we were separated the year before? Was one mad and trying to get me to argue with Kevin so she could get him back? That couldn't be true if he really hadn't seen anyone while we were apart, which is what he'd told me, and I'd believed him.

Since Kevin was working, I texted him as soon as we walked into the house. When I told him what I'd found in the mailbox, he thought it was just a nasty joke and assured me that he'd get the panties himself as soon as he returned home from work. I acted like I was cool about it, but that was only so he wouldn't take the time to figure out a lie to make me feel better, just in case.

That night when Kevin came home from work I had to drill him a little just to make sure he wouldn't be tempted to try and lie to me to cover up for anyone. I needed names of the local females he had seen when we weren't together, and I needed to know how they took it when he'd told them that we were starting over.

And I got nothing.

Kevin just knew that it wasn't any female he knew who'd put underwear in our mailbox. He said he hadn't had a chance to see anyone else while we were separated because we got back together as soon as he was about to take someone on a date.

The way that he was so cut and dry and nonchalant about it left me sort of speechless. I had no good comeback for his response, so I left it alone. Besides, what went on with him when we weren't together really wasn't my business. It would only become my business if I found out someone from his past had put panties in my mailbox.

Maybe it was one of the gorgeous Huck sisters. They were beautiful girls, but maybe they were hiding hatred behind those hazel eyes we all adored. Was one of them crushing on Kevin and I was the last to find out? I didn't want to believe that, but weren't young girls the only females who wore leopard-print thongs those days?

I loved their family, and I think they loved us too. We all got along so well, even inviting each other to cookouts and birthday celebrations throughout the years. The girls even called us "Mr. Kevin" and "Mrs. Dawn" too. That would have been extremely weird for either of the sisters to be crushing on a man she called "mister." Wouldn't it?

Therefore, it couldn't have been one of them, or could it?

4
Not Knowing

The second time the harasser struck was less than six months after the first incident. On December 5, 2013 I realized that I was definitely the one being watched.

The dingy, black and pink panties had been dropped in my mailbox and were balled in the corner underneath the mail. The mail carrier had to have seen them this time, unless she was the harasser. For a split second, I did wonder about her. She had to have seen the panties because she still placed the mail on top of them then closed the receptacle back like there was nothing wrong.

This was getting crazy, and I needed to know whom it was that was doing it so that they could be stopped.

I'd walked to the mailbox this time, so after getting the mail and seeing the surprise, I coolly closed the door, held onto my composure, and turned back around to head across the street and towards my yard. As I waited for a car to pass before I crossed to my side of the street, I did a quick glance to my left and right to see if anyone was there lingering around.

Melissa must've been working onsite today because her car wasn't in the yard. Usually her work-at-home job allowed her to do most tasks from the comfort of her residence, but because the company was local, it was easy for supervisors to call employees into the office when extra work was needed or when visitors were coming into town.

They'd probably called her in again.

This time I would have to go about things differently if I wanted to finally find out who was placing panties in our box. After calling Kevin and telling him it had happened again, I decided to do what most young people in the black neighborhood don't do too often: I called the police.

The officer who responded to my call arrived about thirty minutes later. The way it worked was if you told the 911 operator that you didn't think you were in immediate danger and in need of emergency assistance, then an officer would come out after taking emergency calls first. That was understandable, but I wonder if it's that way in all neighborhoods.

Nevertheless, the officer who responded was a nice guy and also seemed disgusted with what he saw. When I asked about checking the mailbox for fingerprints, he advised me that it wouldn't work since so many people are in and out of our mailbox regularly.

That was a slight blow until he mentioned that it was, however, a federal offense for someone to go into our mailbox. I could contact the postmaster, file a complaint, and there would be an investigation of the incidents. If the person were ever identified then he or she would also have federal charges along with any charges I might file for harassment.

I was so thankful that the officer actually grabbed a pair of gloves before retrieving the panties from my mailbox.

"See," I pointed to the ditch directly behind the mailbox.

"What's that?" The officer could see the gray and black garment balled up in the wet ditch but didn't know what he was looking at.

Not thinking about the fees or consequences of littering, I told him, "Those are the panties from the last time somebody put some in my mailbox. We threw them down there when we realized what they were. We didn't want to take those disgusting things into our house."

"Okay. Well, we'll definitely file these as evidence, but I won't mess with the ones in the ditch since they're all wet."

I didn't blame him. I had already refused to touch them when I told Kevin it had happened again. I didn't care if I had on ten pairs of gloves. I was not touching them.

As we walked back to his truck and continued to talk we realized that we were drawing a lot of attention. It was normal though. Heck, anytime a uniformed officer is at someone's house in a black neighborhood, all attention is on him and the person he is speaking to. Cars that usually flew by were creeping, their drivers staring harder than ever, not caring that we were watching them watching us while they were being nosey. Even my nosey neighbor from across the street was at the back corner of his yard watching the entire time.

"It could be him for all I know," I nodded my head towards the moped-pusher so the officer could see whom I was referring to, "but I doubt it. He's just nosey."

"Okay. You make sure to call if it happens again then." The officer gave me the card with the report number on it and left.

As soon as the officer left, I did a Google search for the contact information for the postal investigator. I wanted to call as soon as possible to report it. This person had to be stopped once and for all.

When I found the closest investigator in Charlotte, I called the number and was surprised to find that I had to leave a voicemail on an automated line. After the prompt was finished, I quickly explained what happened and was sure to mention that I did file a complaint with the police department. I just had to cover every legal action I'd taken in that short voicemail message. I didn't want the investigator to think I was some ghetto chick who was reporting people just for the heck of it or who was doing it to get back at someone out of spite.

The whole ordeal was so embarrassing, and I had no one to tell at that time but my husband and select ones of my closest friends. I had to find out for sure what was going on and who was doing it before I spoke up.

Then I couldn't tell Mommy and my sister Keisha. I just knew that they would worry too much and would urge us to move. If only moving again was that easy. Not when you're an unemployed student.

Sometimes it seemed like my family worried about us too much, but in a good way. Just like when Bryant was a newborn and Lil' Kevin was four years old, if we went to visit them in Dillon, Keisha would check behind me after I'd already fastened them in their car seats. She always said she "just wanted to be sure."

I loved it though.

I'd never told neither Mommy nor Keisha about the

neighborhood guy banging on my door that night. They would've been relieved that Kevin confronted him, but they still would've been worried that the guy would try it again when Kevin went back to work. With all of this constantly plaguing my mind when I talked to my family, I knew I couldn't tell them about the panties incidents until the harassment stopped.

When I called Kevin back, boy, did he give me the news of the century! This wasn't the second time that panties were left for one of us to find them. This was the third time.

According to Kevin, one morning after we'd moved onto McNair Road, he'd walked outside to leave for work, and there was a pair of panties on the driver's side of my Hyundai.

That made it personal.

Everyone knows we've always had separate cars. Kevin barely drove mine. I rarely drove his.

That meant I was the one who was being watched and targeted.

That meant that I possibly had a stalker...

Kevin said when it happened in 2009, he had thought that the young neighborhood boys had done it as a joke. Therefore, he'd simply trashed the panties and never mentioned it. But finding out years later after it happened again made me question every time I'd had that feeling that eyes were on me—times when I'd been outside in the yard and no one was visibly around.

At 5'6" with a slim figure and creamy chocolate skin, I was

enough of an eye-pleaser. I'd received the usual thirsty stares and ridiculous mating call sounds from men visiting people in the neighborhood. Some women love that kind of attention.

I despise it.

The situation was getting too creepy and way too personal. Was there some psychotic woman watching my husband and awaiting her chance to be with him? Or was some jealous man awaiting his opportunity to get me pissed enough with Kevin so he could wiggle his way into my life, all because of a sick lie and some dirty panties?

I was determined to find out.

I heard back from the postal investigator the next day. He told me I'd done the right thing by contacting authorities. He also advised me that he would send me some documents in the mail that I needed to file a federal complaint against the person if his or her identity was ever discovered.

In the meantime, he stated that I had some options in trying to catch the person or in preventing anyone from going into our mailbox. I could set up a camera inside of it that could catch the culprit in action. I could replace our mailbox with one that had a lock on it, or I could simply get a post office box that all of our mail could go to.

The latter of the two would eliminate the panty placements altogether, but the former would mean that I could possibly find out who the culprit was and could have them prosecuted and stopped, hopefully.

The first option was the most appealing, yet the others made me wonder what the consequences would be for me. If the harasser didn't have my mailbox to use as his or her form of harassment, then what would the next option be? Would the person skip the mailbox altogether, cross the street, and then bravely come into the yard? Would our sicko be waiting on me whenever I stepped out of the car on a dark night?

I honestly couldn't answer those questions without doubting the affirmative answers.

After thanking the investigator for the information, I searched online for camera systems. I found every kind you could possibly imagine: the ones that went inside of mailboxes and had night vision capabilities, cameras that could go on top of the house and could be aimed directly at the mailbox, and so many more. They were all way too expensive though.

I figured I might as well use my old-fashioned JVC camcorder and set it up by the window facing the front of the house each time I was leaving home. That would catch my harasser for sure!

Meanwhile, if I was gonna go out, I wasn't gonna let it be an easy task for anyone. After the last incident, I made sure that I carried my stun gun every day. All 200,000 volts would surely protect me. Then the Beretta stayed loaded, and baseball bats were behind the front and back doors.

I wasn't gonna go out without one helluva good fight!

But against whom?

Not knowing who is bothering you is worse than knowing because you don't know the extent of how far you must go to protect yourself and your family, if and when necessary.

Unless it was all a twisted joke.

5

The Neighborhood Thief

Soon I went straight into detective mode. The next time panties were placed in my mailbox, I was going to catch the person putting them there red-handed, have a face-to-face consultation, and then call the police.

I grabbed my camcorder and its charger from off of the top shelf in my closet and searched the house for the perfect spot to set it up. It had to be facing the mailbox, but because it was so old, it would have to stay plugged up the whole time since the battery was dead. Then its short cord would have to be close enough to reach a power outlet.

Each time I used the camcorder I had to keep in mind there was only an hour and a half of recording time left, but I refused to delete any important memories I'd caught on camera: those of my boys as infants; those of Lil' Kevin and my niece, Dollbaby, reading at age three; those of every holiday gathering since receiving the camcorder as a Christmas gift in 2005; and those of our family vacations to the beach. I would never delete those memories.

I found the perfect spot in our bonus room near the desk by the window.

That day when we left and came back home, the first thing I did was check the mailbox. After not discovering any disgusting gifts, I hurried into the house to see what, if any, unusual activity happened while my best friend Cherise and I were off shopping.

Nothing did, so I continued on with my day.

***

It had been a while since the last incident, yet I still recorded each time I left the house, always finding myself deleting the new material from the quiet day.

One day, when Cherise and I'd left the house, Kevin's blue, black, and white Nikes that he did yard work in were on the back steps. I never understood why he wore such nice shoes outside to feed the dog or mow the acre of grass, but all of his shoes were nice. I think it was a sneaker fetish that some guys had, especially those, like him, who received the alerts when the new Jordans came out and therefore, rushed to the shoe store to grab a pair of what he called "classics" that he'd once had in high school.

I didn't quite get it, but that was his thing. I just accepted it.

When Cherise and I returned from shopping, I rushed inside the house and pulled the camcorder from its spot on top of the books I'd stacked on the desk to get the best view of the mailbox. I stopped the recording, then flipped around the screen and clicked the "Play" button to view my last video.

I looked at every single car that rode by my mailbox, waiting for anyone suspicious-looking to creep along the road. Thankfully, I didn't notice anything strange. All I saw on the recording was one of Jerry's stepsons walking by as usual and my neighbor from across the street, walking along minding his business.

I put the camera back down and went along with my day, awaiting the arrival of the bus.

Right before the boys came home I walked to the backdoor and gazed out into the yard. It had really come a long way from the woody forest that used to be behind us leaving little playroom for us to enjoy. I opened the door and inhaled a breath of the fresh, country air, but as I was closing the door, I realized that Kevin's Nikes were gone. I looked around the bottom of the steps then glanced across the yard in case a stray dog had moved them. They were nowhere to be found.

I had to replay the outing with Cherise in my head. Hadn't I seen the shoes before we left, or was my memory deceiving me?

I texted Cherise to ask if she'd seen any shoes on the steps or in the yard before we'd left the house. After realizing she would still be on the road since she lived an hour away, I decided to call her instead, only to find that she couldn't recall if she'd seen them or not.

When I thanked her and called Kevin to ask if he'd moved his shoes, he confirmed what I'd already figured. He said they should've still been out there.

Somebody had to have stolen them!

According to the video, the only two people who had walked by had been my neighbor from across the street and the stepson from the dirt road beside us. Therefore, the thief had to be one of them.

Because of his history of taking things that didn't belong to him, we figured it was the stepson. For that reason, I wanted to speak to him myself before Kevin got home.

Kevin was simply too durn nice. But not me.

I didn't appreciate anyone walking into our yard and taking any belonging of ours. I'd had enough. I was going to get the camera footage and report it to the police. I'd just have to take it to the police station myself, plug the camera up, and play my findings for them.

Well, thank God for a rational husband who keeps me grounded. Kevin didn't want to take the recording to the police because it only showed the stepson walking by the road in front of our house and then turning to go down the dirt road to head home.

He was the only one in that short time frame, but because we didn't have another camera facing the backyard, it would be hard to prove with 100% certainty that he was the culprit.

Still, Kevin planned to settle it by talking to the parents whenever he saw them. That was the responsible thing to do. That's what I'd want to happen if my boys did anything. Tell me. Don't try to confront my children.

Not mine.

The young man wasn't actually a child although he was still someone's child. He had been in prison before and was supposed to have been getting his life together. I'd admired that and was actually proud of him for trying to make a positive change. Kevin was proud of him too when his stepdad had told him the good news.

Months later, Kevin just didn't like the fact that the guy had stole his shoes when all he had to do was ask for them. He had even offered to help get the young man a job. But on the day he was supposed to come by to go over some tips on getting through to a particular hiring manager of a local company, the young man never showed.

Every day for the next two weeks, I looked out of the blinds whenever I heard a male's voice. I was waiting on the brother or anyone else to walk by with the Nikes on. I was going to confront him (because I knew it had to be one of the neighborhood guys) and make him give them back.

It was all about the principle...

I hadn't thought very far ahead on how I was going to make a grown man do anything, but I had to say something so it wouldn't happen again.

Of course, that didn't happen. I didn't see either of the stepsons at all for the next two weeks, and I didn't see anyone walking by with the shoes on.

One Saturday, I brought it up in a conversation with Kevin who dropped the bomb on me when he said that just that morning he'd seen the other brother walking down the dirt road wearing his stolen shoes. I could not believe the nerve of the thief. I hopped up from my spot at the table when he said that.

"Girl, sit down." Kevin looked at me and smirked a little. He knew how fiery my temper could be. "I talked to him, and he claimed that he has some just like mine, so I told him to bring me his shoebox then. You see he ain't been back up here."

"I'm so tired of people coming in our yard!" I had had enough.

This wasn't the first time.

There had been several missing items from our yard over the years since we'd first moved there in 2009: the green Lowe's weed eater that we couldn't get to crank, Lil' Kevin's red bicycle that had a chain that couldn't seem to stay fixed, our shovel with the splinter-filled wooden pole…all sorts of items. And we never caught the person who did it.

The neighborhood thief was pretty good at what he did. He hit other houses too.

In December of 2013 Melissa ordered her son's sneakers for Christmas, and they were scheduled for delivery at her house one morning. According to UPS, the driver left the box on her front porch, so shortly after getting her confirmation that the shoes were delivered, Melissa went home to check on the shipment but only to find that the shoes had disappeared.

When she called me, she asked if I'd seen anyone near her house. Unfortunately, from inside of my house, I couldn't see her front porch or front yard at all because of the trees between our houses.

For the remainder of the day, I stayed on the lookout for any suspicious person with new kicks on. I was going to call Melissa immediately and let her know the direction the person had headed.

Strangely enough, I never saw anyone on foot at all that day. And those shoes were never found. Our neighborhood thief seemingly saw all and knew of all our comings and goings throughout the day.

But was the neighborhood thief the same person who was leaving panties in our mailbox?

6

The Abandoned House

Days and weeks of absolutely nothing passed. I found myself leaving the house on purpose just to catch the pervert on video red-handed, but to no avail. I still recorded each time I was away from the house and had to erase each recording after viewing it so the camcorder would be ready to catch my mailbox during the next outing.

I could not ever slip up. If I did, there's no telling how long the harassment would continue, especially with it going on for much longer than I'd even known.

Although panties hadn't been placed in my mailbox in a while, something strange did happen at Terry's vacant house to the right of us.

When we first moved to McNair Road, we'd always see Terry while we were outside in the yard playing ball. And each time he saw us, he'd yell out, "Hey, Neighbors!" and we'd yell the same.

The boys called him "Mr. Terry" and really took a liking to his politeness. Quite frankly, we all did, but the rumor on our street was that he was an alcoholic and former drug addict, and that's why he was missing front teeth.

I wasn't too sure about the truth behind those rumors, and it wasn't my business to find out either. I did, however, forbid my boys from going to his house or doing much more than speaking to him and only while Kevin and I were around.

It was nothing personal.

Scratch that.

It was very personal.

It was that way with everyone. If you didn't have kids the same age or close to the same age as my boys, and I hadn't grown to know you personally, then my sons would not be spending any time with you.

For what reason anyway?

There is no reason for our sons and daughters to be placed under the care or company of a stranger. *Yes, I said "stranger." Now let that truth set into your soul and set you free.*

I will never understand why some parents trust so easily and allow their children to be around undercover perverts who they aren't even familiar with themselves. Some parents don't even know the last name, let alone the real first name, of the newest babysitter who overly states how much they "love children." That should be the first hint of weirdness, yet the sick tendencies and lack of knowledge about the so-called "children lover" are often still overlooked, to the detriment of the innocent child.

Then the clueless parent is the first one wanting to kill the pervert for sexually abusing the babies as soon as he or she drops them off at the sicko's house and barely gets halfway around the block.

Not me. And not my children.

After realizing that we hadn't seen Terry in a long time, the other rumor that I heard was that he was extradited to New York for murder charges dating back from when he was a young man some thirty odd years ago. It was unfortunate because he didn't seem like the cold-blooded murder type at all. No, not Terry.

Terry seemed so kind-hearted and willing to help anybody...

***

The last time we had a big cookout at our house in 2011 we asked Terry if he wanted something to eat. Besides, he lived alone, and we had plenty of food to share.

Well, we thought he lived alone until one of his Mexican

friends came walking outside and stood behind him. When we were giving Terry his plate of barbecued food, he thanked us, but before walking away, he asked if we had any extra that he could get for his "friends" too.

"Friends" is plural.

Almost as if "friends" was the signal word, the screen door of Terry's house swung open, and about thirty more smiling Mexicans walked out, heading straight towards us.

I hadn't remembered seeing all of those men in that house or on the back of the pickup truck that took Terry to work every morning when it wasn't raining.

It was simply amazing.

As the "friends" headed our way, Terry told me that they worked with him doing construction and were living there until they had enough money saved up to get back home to their families in Central America. I found it to be quite chivalrous. A man doing his best to take care of his family is to be duly noted on any day.

So two of my girls and I walked back to my house, grabbed some loaves of bread, loaded a bunch of paper plates with chicken, hot dogs, and hamburgers, as well as a plate full of sides, and headed back to Terry and friends. We may not have understood much of what they said when we handed over the food, other than "gracias," but their glistening eyes, sincere smiles, and constant nods said it all.

***

When Terry sort of disappeared a few months later and was rumored to not be returning, I noticed that some guy on a red bike had been sneaking inside through the backdoor when he thought no one had noticed. I think he was probably over there smoking weed although I never actually smelled any. Who knows?

I couldn't figure out what other reason he would have to be going in there when he thought we weren't home or when our blinds were closed as if we were asleep. It wasn't my business, so I didn't look any further into it.

Then, there was another twenty-something-year-old guy from down the road. This one would sometimes be in Terry's overgrown front yard talking to Terry's other friends and family members as if Terry were actually in the house. After a few days of him going back and sneaking into the house when no one was around and coming out a few minutes later, I didn't see him again.

Who knows what he had been doing in there.

Since Terry pretty much vanished into thin air, and after realizing that people could sneak in and out of his abandoned house any time they chose, every few months I began checking to see if his property taxes had been paid. As soon as taxes became delinquent and went to public auction, I wanted to buy the property from the delinquent tax sale. Then, the plan was to bulldoze the house.

Unfortunately for us, someone kept paying the taxes right before they became fully delinquent and were sent to the sale. It was probably the older woman from the house on the right side of his. Supposedly, she's his aunt...

***

What really made me want to get rid of the house was the incident that happened at the beginning of 2014, which was just weeks after someone had placed the last pair of panties in our mailbox.

One afternoon when I arrived home, I followed the gravel path to the backyard and saw a man on the back steps of Terry's house. I knew it wasn't either of the previous younger guys I'd seen there, but I couldn't tell whom it was that was standing there with that hat and tan jacket on. As I crept closer to the patch of grass right next to the dirt road that was between our two houses, it became clearer and clearer that it was a short, dark-skinned man.

I don't think he saw me coming, and it wasn't because a great distance was between us. It was because he was in a trancelike state and probably *couldn't* see me. He was too involved with flicking his hand back and forth and staring straight out into the distance. His arm moved faster and faster, and I felt more and more nervous.

As I sat in the car with its tinted windows still rolled, I could feel my body begin to tremor.

Breathe, Dawn, just breathe.

I inhaled and moved the gear to "park" before reaching for my pocketbook. Mommy told me to always have my stun gun in my hand as I came and went at night. She'd told me that without even knowing about the mailbox incidents. Once I could feel the bulky, rectangular shape at the bottom of my pocketbook, I finally released my breath.

It was time to get out.

I grabbed my cell phone and speed dialed Kevin.

"Hello? What's up, Boo?" Thank God he answered!

"Boo…I just pulled up and some man is on the back steps of Terry's yard. I think he's masturbating!" My voice was trembling a bit, but I managed to clearly get my words out.

"What? *Masturbating?*" I'm sure Kevin sat all the way up in his desk chair to hear the answer on the other end of the phone line.

"Yes! I'm in the car about to run in the house. I see his hand moving back and forth, but it's like he's in a trance and didn't even notice me pulling up. Hold on, let me try to record it!"

I looked at the phone and turned the speaker on before mistakenly clicking the camera button and taking a picture.

"Durn it!" Realizing I wasn't actually recording, I then hit the video button, aimed the phone back at the man, and waited.

"Are you going in the house?" Kevin was still there.

"Oh, yeah. He's still just doing the same thing. I'm recording him."

"Dawn, stop recording, and just run in the house real quick, but keep me on the phone. Apparently, he doesn't see you."

"Okay. Hold on." I turned the phone and clicked on the "play" button, but only to find that the man's face couldn't be made out because of how dark the recording was. "Oh my gosh! It's too durn dark! Ugh!"

"Just go in the house, Dawn. That man won't hardly bother you, but keep me on the phone now." Kevin sounded calm, yet firm, and was trying to also sound nonchalant, probably so I wouldn't panic.

I bet he was tired of these calls from his scary wife. Heck, I was tired of having these crazy incidents. I'd rather have a full-time first-shift job and not have to deal with any of the mess I was dealing with while being at home when Kevin wasn't there.

"Okay."

I took the phone off of speaker, tilted my head to the left, and tucked the phone between my left ear and shoulder. I threw my pocketbook on my right arm and slid the stun gun into my hand, just in case. I don't think I've ever hopped out of the car so fast in life, and as I moved, I kept my eyes on the man who still hadn't noticed my presence. Apparently, he was way too into his daydreams to realize I'd pulled up in the yard and was getting out of the car to head in the house.

By the time I got into the backdoor and ran to the kitchen window, the man was almost racing up the dirt road. I followed his steps around the inside of my house, now peeping from my den window that looked out to the road in front of my mailbox. The man crossed the street after letting a speeding car pass and went straight to my neighbor's house.

"Hey, he's gone to our neighbor's house!" I told Kevin.

He never left my side when I needed him.

Remembering the video recording in the bonus room, I got off of the phone after letting Kevin know I would check the camcorder to see who the man was. I knew it wasn't the nasty-looking man I'd had problems with in the past; I would've easily recognized him. This time, it was someone else.

I rushed into the bonus room where I had the camcorder staged, went to the video, and pressed "Play." I fast-forwarded the speed times fifteen to more quickly see who was headed to the abandoned house. After a few seconds, the same guy in the tan jacket and cap was walking past my house and toward my mailbox with his hands in his pockets.

When I slowed down the video, I could see the man pausing to let a white car pass. Then he looked back towards our house and crossed the street, heading to Terry's abandoned house. I paused the video and zoomed in on the man's face, but to my realization, it was just Jerome—my nosey neighbor who lived across the street directly in front of Melissa.

7
The Dillon in Me

After two months of no surprises in the mailbox, I began to feel as though I'd never find out the identity of the person who was leaving the panties. Had she or he moved away?

I knew that the young boy who usually walked the neighborhood streets had been walking by less and less, and one of the stepsons was doing well and had moved in with his uncle who'd gotten him a job working alongside of him.

If it was a love-struck woman who'd put undies in our mailbox, had she finally moved on and gotten a man of her own? I would never be the same if I didn't know.

The video recording had failed me. Or, shall I say, I had failed to get my answer by relying on the camcorder. What else could I possibly do when every other method had failed me?

Pray.

I began to pray and ask God to reveal the person who had been harassing me. After more days of nothing, deep inside it felt like part of my prayer was answered since I hadn't discovered any more panties in my mailbox. I still didn't know who the person was, but I couldn't rush God in showing me either. The old folks in Dillon always said, "In due time, he'll reveal your enemies."

I waited, thinking time was definitely due, but I slipped up. I stopped recording each time I left the house. I don't know what within me changed and made me think that it was okay to stop the recordings. Maybe it was because after a while I felt that it was actually over because of how quiet things were.

Well, it wasn't over.

On February 27, 2014, the harasser struck again. It was as if I had been slapped and spit on. How could I have been so stupid to think it was okay to not set up the camcorder?

I'd always been told that God helps those who help themselves and that faith without work is dead. I've always known it to be true, so how could I have been so confident that He would reveal the person who was doing it when I had stopped doing my part in trying to catch him or her on camera?

At first, I just knew that I had failed myself. I just knew that I would never catch the person. We were going to have to move in order for the harassment to stop…just walk away from our home that we loved and start over someplace else.

Purchasing a home wasn't a task that came easily for us, let alone any young couple with a family. Kevin and I hadn't been paying on our house long enough to have accumulated much equity, and the few home improvements we'd done wouldn't have amounted to much yet anyway. In order for us to move, we'd have to first sell our house and would have to pull money from all over just to do it. Then I would have to have been on a new job for at least a year for a bank to even think about financing us. I was still out of work, so that was out of the question.

Options were few, but I am so thankful that I was blessed with a mother who told me that there was always that one option that could fix things when no other option could do it. And for my whole life, I had that crazy faith in God that carried me through everything. And I mean everything.

Jesus had worked for me growing up, so I knew He would work for me as an adult too. I just had to revert to having that strong faith in God that my harasser would be caught and stopped. Through faith, actions, and steadfast prayers, I was not going to give up.

On February 27, I had a sense of normalcy going on in my life.

I had a regular routine and had to run a tight shift as a full-time online student, housewife, and baseball mom. At 9:15 that morning I received a text from Advanced Dental Center to remind me about my appointment at 11:15, so instead of me trying to take a quick nap after dropping the boys off to school, like I often did, I decided to stay up. I did my usual cleaning and some schoolwork before heading out at 11:00.

I just loved how convenient it was to go to my dentist's office. It was only ten minutes away, and their service was always quick. Like any other day, I was back home within the next hour.

When I pulled onto McNair Road and got closer to my mailbox, I realized that I didn't want to have to walk back across the yard in my heels. And I didn't want to have to change just to check the mail. I decided to go ahead and pull up in the car and check it.

And there they were.

The multi-colored pink, black, and white panties were scrunched up in my mailbox, looking like they belonged to some little girl.

The other times that I'd found underwear in my box felt different. On the surface, it went from feeling like a joke in the very beginning to now feeling as if someone pissed off or really lonely was behind it. And for this to be going on for so long, it seemed as though someone sick had to be involved.

Where in the world had these panties come from? Did they belong to a young girl who had been raped and victimized by a sicko? Did they belong to a woman who had been kidnapped and violated, or had the panties been stolen from a store or someone's house? I didn't know, but something had to change before someone got hurt.

I immediately called 911 again. I let the operator know that someone had placed panties in our mailbox before and that I'd previously reported it. As usual, since I was in no immediate danger the operator advised me that they would send someone soon.

This time I decided to carefully think it through. I had only been gone for an hour, my usual timeframe, so any close neighbor should remember seeing someone on the street within that short period.

Melissa!

I grabbed my cell and scrolled to our last text messaging conversation and clicked on the phone icon to dial her number. Her car wasn't in her driveway, but maybe she'd only been gone for a short amount of time. I had to calm myself before she picked up. She'd never heard me like this before.

"Hello?" Whew, she answered!

"Hey, Melissa. Did you see anybody walking down the road today within the past hour?"

"Hey. Um, yeah, I saw Jerome walking earlier. Why? What's wrong?"

"I found panties in my mailbox. Wait. *Jerome?* Which way was he heading?" I was all ears now.

"Oh gosh...he went walking towards your mailbox. Then I looked, and he was heading back to his house and went in."

"Was he on the same side of the road as my mailbox?"

Melissa paused for a split second before answering, "Yeah, he was."

"Oh my gosh! That freakin' pervert! Then he's the one who's been puttin' panties in my mailbox!" I could barely control my words at that moment.

At least I wasn't crying like I wanted to.

I could not believe it. All this time…it had to be him. No one else was on the road for that short period, and why would he be near my mailbox?

It had to be Jerome.

"Wow, that's crazy! But, yep, he's the only one I saw walking that way this morning before I left." Melissa confirmed it, but how could I prove it? I wasn't about to let him get away with this, whether I had evidence or not. I was going to stop him, and I was going to do it today.

It had to be Jerome, right?

Whomever it was saw me coming and going every time I left

the house. He or she had to have seen me at the window setting up the camcorder for them to know what days to not go near my mailbox. The perv had to have known Kevin's schedule too. The person never did it when Kevin wasn't working or at times he would have been checking the mail himself. Heck, the harasser never touched our mailbox on days when Kevin was home, period. The person had to have been that nosey and that sick too.

The nosey sicko had to be Jerome.

Melissa told me she was on her way back home in a few minutes and said that she could come over and tell the police what she saw. But the Dillon in me wanted to confront Jerome face to face. I had to show him for myself that I knew what was going on and that I didn't find it to be funny.

I opened the wooden front door and pushed it all the way against the wall behind it so I could see across the street. Jerome was there, standing by the back corner of his yard, in the same spot he'd been in when I'd pulled up to my mailbox. He had no idea what was heading his way. I might be 5'6" and skinny as hell, but I would fight a stalking grown man if I had to.

I picked up my cell and speed-dialed Kevin, who thankfully, answered his phone. I calmly, or as calmly as I could, let him know what had happened—again. Kevin doesn't usually anger very easily. He's the type of person who stays out of family arguments that don't concern him, and he's the type who also keeps his opinion to himself unless asked for it.

This time was different.

Kevin wanted to go over to Jerome's as soon as he got off work. But he was short-staffed and couldn't leave the credit union he managed. At the time, I was unemployed and didn't have much to lose if I were to get into any legal trouble for confronting a pervert, but because Kevin did have a lot to lose, including his job and reputation, I made him promise that he would let me handle things legally. The police would be arriving any minute.

There was only one thing that Kevin asked me to not do, or shall I say, "told me" to not do: confront Jerome myself.

Sorry.

I let my husband know that that was exactly what I was going to do. He couldn't change my mind. He did, however, get me to agree that I would keep him on the phone on a muted speaker while I went over to Jerome's.

Cherise had already called earlier that morning to let me know that she was in Florence and would be stopping by before she headed back to her house in Kingstree, which was an hour away. I called her and told her to slow down before stopping by because I had something to do right quick.

She was almost at the house already, so I tried to wait a second to let her inside. In the meantime, I changed out of my heels and into some comfortable high-top sneakers. I was ready and not in the mood to wait longer than a minute, so I headed to the front of the house.

When I entered the den, I could hear Cherise's Cadillac truck crunching across the gravel driveway and circling around the back of the house. I ran and unlocked the back wooden door and opened the screen door. When she hopped out the truck and came and sat at the kitchen table, the first things she noticed were the Beretta I'd placed on the table and my sneakers.

"Um...Dawn, girl what is going on? Why you got the gun out? And why do you have on sneakers? You never wear sneakers." As one of my closest friends, Cherise always noticed everything.

Everything.

She knew that I only wore sneakers on three occasions: when I was at one of the boys' sports games or practices, when I was playing in the yard with them, or when I was ready to fight as a last resort. There was no game or practice going on at that time of day, and no one was outside playing in the yard.

***

The last time I'd worn sneakers to fight was a few months before I'd gotten laid off from the home mortgage company. When I was fed up with two females from another department for constantly looking at me and laughing, I went in to work one morning suited up in jeans, a t-shirt, and sneakers. I usually wore professional attire, like a cute blouse, dress pants, and heels.

That day I didn't want anyone to deter me from busting one of those chicks in the mouth, so I didn't say anything to my friends until after I'd gone to confront the girls. God was with me and maybe even with them that day because miraculously they wouldn't even look my way.

I had gone as far as waiting on one of them to go to lunch and had followed her outside and stood right beside her, just waiting on an incorrect look my way. It never happened. Surprisingly, from that day forward, the two avoided all eye contact with me. In fact, I never saw them look my way or even attempt to giggle at all when I was walking by again.

All I can say is God will stop your enemy when you pray...

***

"Dawn! I said, 'what's going on?'" Cherise brought me out of my daydreams.

"Oh, I'll tell you in a minute. I'm going across the street right quick to talk to my neighbor, and the police are on the way here."

"What?" Poor Cherise had no clue what was going on in my head or what I was about to do.

"I'll tell you about it when I get back. Just stay inside, okay?" I did not want anyone I loved and cared about to be involved in what could turn into a messy situation.

"Oh, okay…" She seemed confused, yet she seemed to understand how serious I was. I saw her grab her cell, probably to call her husband Brian, and I grabbed mine to call Kevin.

I picked up the Beretta and flipped it over to see if the red light was showing. It was, but I couldn't remember if that meant it was on or off of safety. I didn't want to take any chances. The last time I'd had to pull the gun out for protection had been bad enough.

8
Not Falling for it

On one particular afternoon, I was at home alone while the boys were in school and Kevin was at work. When I heard a knock on the back door, I instantly became infuriated.

We very rarely had visitors unless they'd called ahead of time. Melissa and her family were at work and school—like normal people would be during the middle of a workday. The youngest Huck children were in school with our boys, the older sons never came to our house at all, and their parents wouldn't be stopping by during the day because the husband worked and the wife was disabled.

My family would have let me know that they were in town, let alone headed to my house. My friends were all working too, and the majority of them lived out of town anyway.

That meant that there was only one strong possibility of who the knocker might be: the nasty-looking man who always seemed to bother me when Kevin wasn't at home. It had to be him. We had already warned him to not come on our property again. Yet, here he was again trying me when Kevin wasn't around. I had to take a stand and show him it didn't matter if I was alone or with my protector.

I could, and would, defend myself.

I kicked my furry bedroom shoes off and ran to the bedroom, grabbing the Beretta before running back to the door where the knocker was still waiting. Holding the gun in my right hand, I quickly unlocked the top, then bottom locks on the door and slung it open. There stood the disgusting neighborhood pervert with his tank top halfway pulled up, staring at me like he wanted to rip me apart.

I turned and slapped the gun on top of the dryer, then grabbed the baseball bat and snatched the lock off of the screen door. When I pressed the door handle and clicked it open, I raised the bat then placed the end of it up against the nuisance's head.

"Didn't I tell you to stay the hell away from here?" I pressed the bat deeper against his head as he began to walk backwards down the steps.

"Yes, ma'am!" The guy acted apologetic for a moment and pulled completely away from the bat and began to jog away.

I knew it was only an act so he wouldn't get hit.

"I told you to stay away from here! Don't bring your ass in my yard!" I took off right behind him as he ran towards the second driveway next to Melissa's house, keeping my distance in case he decided to try and take me on.

"Yes, ma'am!" he continued to run until he'd reached the road and I'd finally stopped following.

I'd had enough of him. Even after chasing him away, I had to do more. I needed for it to be on record that he was harassing me. What if he came back again? He was already coming onto our property after we'd advised him not step on it again.

I called the police to report the pervert for coming onto our property after being warned not to. I quickly mentioned that I'd actually chased him away with a weapon this time. Somebody had to do something. I was tired of being bothered while in my own house. Your house is supposed to be your safe haven, your fortress, just as our white stone house was growing up in Dillon.

The craziest part was when the officer arrived and went to look for the pervert whose name I still didn't know then. I looked out the front window minutes later, and there he was, swiftly walking by the road in front of my house. And as he walked, he looked directly towards my den as my blinds were still cracked open.

How the heck could the officer not have run into him? Then again, the pest did always seem to disappear into the thin country air after harassing me.

I didn't even bother to call the cops back.

Taking matters into my own hands, I called Melissa to see if she'd, by chance, seen what had happened since the guy went running towards my driveway, which was connected to her yard by a set of trees. Although she hadn't witnessed it, she was able to give me a name for the one neighborhood pest who fit my description: Lionel Davis.

After learning Lionel's real name, which was totally different from the name "Scott" that he'd given me in the past, I got on the laptop and pulled up the Internet to do a search for any info on him since I'd never seen him on the SLED site as a sex offender. I went straight to the Florence County Detention Center's website to search for any previous booking photos. And there it all was: an extensive timeline of booking photos from several years of arrest history.

But there was an obvious trait that I noticed as I scrolled through the rows of photos. There had been a shift from normal-looking, younger mug shots of Lionel to the more recent ones that showed a steady downturn in his facial appearance and bodily build. Right before my eyes, he went from a healthy, athletic young adult to a perverted-looking, unhealthy man.

I'd witnessed a similar change before, so I had a feeling I knew exactly what the problem was or might have been. If he wasn't on drugs or wasn't an alcoholic, then he had been the victim of what people called "getting laced" or smoking a blunt spiked with embalming fluid.

Through the years in Dillon, there had been several regular, usually popular guys I'd gone to high school with who had been the victims of laced weed. When those guys got laced it usually happened when they were out of town smoking weed with guys who were probably secretly jealous of them and wanted to harm them.

Any ride through the town of Dillon today, you might see one of the victims walking down the road, talking to himself or acting erratically. Some days he might remember who you are, while other days it might be like he has never known you. Some of their facial appearances changed too, making them look older than they actually are. But most were considered harmless.

***

After standing there and thinking for a second, I placed the gun on top of the refrigerator. I did not want to go to jail. Jail would never be the place for me.

I needed to let God fight this one with me without me trying to fire a gun or swing one of our metal baseball bats at anyone. I'd never had to do either of the two before...

I dialed Kevin and headed across the street where Jerome was still standing at the corner of his yard, this time pretending to be doing something with a dog I never knew he had back there.

"Hey, Jerome?" I hopped across the small ditch separating his front yard and the road and called him out.

"Boo, hold on." Thankfully, Kevin answered the line on the first ring. "I'm almost at Jerome's right now."

"Ugh..." Kevin didn't want to hear me ignoring his requests when he was unable to be there to protect me, but I had to take this stand on my own.

Apparently, my harasser liked it that way anyway.

As the short, almost midget-looking man in a tan jacket approached me, for the first time I could actually see his face very clearly. He was an older man and had an almost innocent, child-like demeanor, but I wasn't falling for it. This was a grown, sick man who knew what he was doing, just like the other pervert from the neighborhood.

Jerome and I had never been formally introduced as neighbors. That didn't occur too often in the black neighborhood. No woman or man ever went to the new neighbors, greeting them with a basket of fresh home-baked goodies. Kevin had introduced himself before we moved in, but he didn't remember names. And when he had met the group of males at Jerome's house, it was younger guys that he'd seen that day. Heck, the way that guys used to come and go at Jerome's house, I never really knew who lived there until he and the teenage boy were the only ones left after the old man was gone.

All I knew was that after seeing the ambulance over there a couple of times, I looked one day and the old man was on a stretcher being wheeled out of the house. There was no white sheet covering his face, so he was still alive when he left, but that was the last I had seen him.

"Hey. Yes ma'am?" Jerome's soft voice actually matched his demeanor, but I wasn't falling for that either.

"Jerome, did you walk down the road about an hour ago this morning?" I had to trick him to see if he'd lie.

"Oh, no. I been in my yard all day." He answered so fast, just like a liar would.

The nerve of this pervert.

"So, you're tellin' me you didn't leave your yard at all this morning?" The temperature of my blood just had to be steadily increasing…didn't seem too far away from reaching 200 degrees.

"N-no, I just went and got my mail and came back to my yard."

When someone starts stuttering after you ask them a question, chances are it's because they're lying or are about to try to lie. Why would Jerome be lying about not walking down the street? I already knew the answer, and that's when my boiling point was reached.

"Yes, you did!" My feistiness probably caught him off guard.

"Why you been putting underwear in my mailbox? I know it's you because somebody saw you by my mailbox when it happened, and I called the police. They are on the way!"

"Now I don't bother nobody—I ain't put nothin' in your mailbox! They lyin'!"

"Well, Melissa saw you and she's on her way to let the police know it was you." I said that, rolled my eyes, then turned away, leaving him standing there looking guilty and embarrassed at being called out.

But as I got closer and closer to my porch steps I could hear him mumbling. This time his tone was completely different.

"Man! I don't fuckin' bother no damn body!"

"What? What did you say?" Turning around, I started in the direction of my lying stalker once again. I had no protection with me at all, and I didn't know what I was about to do, but I picked up speed to get to his face as fast as I could.

He really didn't know me like that.

Yet, I inched closer to the road and slowed for a creeping car to pass on by before I headed back to his yard.

"What you say, Jerome?"

Mumbling ever so quietly, Jerome finally shut the hell up and inched away, heading towards the back of his house. He didn't know me to try and curse at me and think I was going to take it.

I wasn't raised that way.

***

It was in our blood to protect ourselves but only when someone messed with us first. We got that from our grandparents, so it was fairly easy to see how it traveled down from each generation.

Even though I'd never seen my mama get into a physical fight with anyone, I'd seen her almost get into one with my six-foot-something uncle one day when I was in college. As heated as she was, she probably would've won too. There's nothing like an older sibling putting her foot down and showing the younger sibling who's the boss.

That day, my then new boyfriend Kevin and I had gone to Dillon to visit my mom when my Uncle C. had arrived. Mommy loved her siblings, and she especially had a soft spot in her heart for her younger brother. He could be so sweet and entertaining, especially when he wasn't drinking.

When Uncle C. turned to ask Kevin for a ride across town, Mommy quickly told him "No" and added that he couldn't ask her guest for a ride in an area he didn't even know in the first place.

Well, Uncle C. didn't want to take that "No" for his final answer from his big sister, so Kevin spoke up and respectfully declined. That still wasn't good enough. Uncle C. went on to try and reason with Kevin on how it wouldn't take long to drop him off at his nearby destination. And that's when Mommy reiterated that Uncle C. shouldn't be asking. And that's when Uncle C. began to get loud and attempted to get irate. *Notice the word "attempted."*

I never understood what made some men think that they could shush and control a woman with a simple deepening of the voice and a louder tone. My mama hadn't taught her three daughters to give in to any man who thought he could talk to us recklessly. Situations like this were the ones in which we'd have to stand our firmest and demand our respect.

Uncle C. must've forgotten that the same fighting people who'd raised him had also raised his older sister. By the fire I saw ignite in my mama's eyes as she arose from that chair, walked over to my uncle, and slapped her hands on her hips, I knew it was about to go down in our living room.

It was upsetting me that this was Kevin's first time even meeting Uncle C. Talk about one heck of a first impression! That was almost the worst thing that could have happened. Just imagine: boyfriend meets new girlfriend's drunken uncle and immediately dumps her. Because I was still in the impressing phase, I wasn't about to screw up my wonderful relationship with my new boo. But my uncle was trying my mama and trying my religion that day!

I guess he must've forgotten about the story of David and Goliath, which I grew up living by. That was another biblical story

Mommy read to us as kids when she taught us about not fearing bullies or people who tried to intimidate us because they may have been bigger in size. I am quite sure that my uncle had been told that very story plenty of times before.

Well Mommy became the strong David that day. She didn't have to shoot Uncle C. with a slingshot, but her words and demeanor were enough to usher him right out that front door. Even when he assumed that he could stand in our yard and argue her down, she stood firmly on our concrete porch, hands still on hips letting him know that he'd better get away from her house and that she would not be moved.

Well, Uncle C. must've gotten the picture, because he never came back to our house that drunk or disrespectful again. And when he did come back, the incident was never mentioned again, just like it had never happened.

That's the way it should be when dealing with relatives. Simply straighten them out when they do wrong and then move on from it. It's only different when you're dealing with disrespectful strangers.

9

The Jacket

As I walked across the yard, up the steps, and through the front door, I almost forgot that I had Kevin on the muted cell phone, listening.

"Boo, did you hear him? He knows he's lying."

"Yeah, I heard him. He's lucky I can't leave from up here, but I'll see him when I get off work."

"No! The police are on the way, Boo. Let's just let them do their job. You know it's probably the only way to stop somebody like him for good."

"Hmm. Okay, we'll see."

Kevin agreed to not say anything to Jerome. But by far, this was the angriest I'd ever heard my husband or ever wanted to hear him. It was kind of sexy though. There's nothing like a man who is willing to protect his family.

When I got inside the house, Cherise was still sitting at the table but this time with her phone in her hand. When I walked over, she stood up, concern flashing in her eyes.

"Okay, now what is going on?" She got right to the point.

"Well, I don't remember if I told you this or not, but a few months ago somebody started putting panties in our mailbox, apparently for me to find them. Sometimes, during broad daylight I'd leave the house and come back, and I'd find them there whenever I checked the mail. Well, today I found out it was my neighbor from across the street who's been doing it."

"What the world?" Cherise always had a way with words.

"Yes, it was that one over there." I walked her to the front door where I still had the heavy wooden door open, leaving the locked screen door for me to look out and watch for Jerome's movement as I waited on the police to arrive.

"That white house right there." I pointed at Jerome's house but only to see him closing his front door and heading down the steps.

"Hold up. He changed his jacket. he just had on a tan one."

Jerome was now wearing a dark-colored jacket.

"And he put on a hat! Oh my goodness, Cherise, I think he's

gonna try and run!"

"Girl, where's he going to run on a moped?" Cherise gave a slight chuckle.

I had to catch myself from also laughing at the thought of a grown man on a moped trying to speed away from a police car.

"Lord, please let the police hurry. I hope that's not what he's about to try to do. Now that would be ridiculous."

While Cherise and I stood there watching, what I feared became the reality of the situation. Jerome walked straight down his steps and looked around him before hopping onto the back of the moped. Cranking it up, he peeped to his left and right, more than likely to be sure that no cars were coming. He then proceeded down the road with the wind slowly whipping on his jacket.

You would've thought he was on a motorcycle with the way he was almost leaning over the handles of that thing with his back slouched like he was a real biker.

Cherise and I just stood there for a minute, mouths gaped and pupils popping in disbelief at my neighbor fleeing the scene on his moped.

For a minute, not only was I speechless, but I also didn't know what to do. My disbelief soon turned into panic. Then my panicking turned into a quick pacing across the small den floor. Should I call 911 back and tell them Jerome was fleeing?

Or was I supposed to run behind him? I'm sure I could've caught up with that moped and snatched the back of his jacket to knock him off and then hold him down until they got there.

That only happened on TV though.

"Should we go after him in the car?" I was the first to break the silence.

"Dawn, no. If you go, then I have to go too, and we can't go chasing behind him when the police are coming!"

"Oh my gosh! But what if he gets away?"

"Girl, where's he gonna go to on that slow thing? You already called the police, so they'll probably run right into him. You gotta wait."

Cherise was right. He couldn't get too far anyway, or at least I hoped not. But only if the police would hurry!

Lord please let the police hurry and catch him! Please, Lord! Please don't let him get away with this!

If I knew of nothing else that I could do, I knew that I had to pray.

"Where in the world are the police?" Cherise broke the new silence first after what felt like another hour had passed. In reality, it was probably only another minute.

"If it's a non-threatening call, they'll wait until they've handled life-threatening ones first."

"Wow, so you mean to tell me we gotta sit here and wait? But he is gone on a moped! Of all things, a *moped!*" Cherise folded her arms into in each other and shook her head, probably from feeling my frustrations and fears too.

Lord, please let the police hurry! Please don't let Jerome get away! Please, Jesus...

I exhaled a huge breath as the heaviness of my burden kept tugging at my body, pulling me down like a crashed car sinking and slowly filling with water. It was getting too late, and Jerome was gone...

Finally, a white and green police Charger pulled into my driveway. It was almost like a Christmas miracle! I could have kissed that officer. By that time, Jerome had only been gone for about three minutes, so maybe the officer had passed him on the road. He was coming from the same direction Jerome had been heading.

I rushed past Cherise, who was still standing at the front screen door with folded arms. As I reached for the door handle, she spoke up, "Hey, I know the cop's here, but I'll wait here with you. I am not leaving you here by yourself with Kevin still at work."

"Thanks, Cherise. I really appreciate it." I had to catch myself from tearing up. I needed that support...

I ran to the driver's side of the officer's car then backed up for him to open his door. When he stepped out of the car, I almost forgot about Jerome. The officer was a tall, well-built man with light brown eyes and a bald head. He looked like he didn't play games.

"Hello, Ma'am, were you the one who called?"

"Yes sir. I'm Dawn."

"Hey. You called about somebody harassing you, and you say it's your neighbor?"

"Oh, yes sir. His name is Jerome. I found out a few minutes ago that he's the one who's been leaving panties in my mailbox, and he did it again today. He lives in that house right there." I pointed at his house, which was directly in front of Melissa's.

"I found out from my other neighbor Melissa. She lives right there." I paused and pointed at Melissa's house to my left before adding, "She said he walked towards my mailbox this morning then turned back around and went back to his yard. He was the only one walking down the road for that short time I was gone, and Melissa saw him. She'll be home in a few minutes. She's going to come by."

"So, he's done this before?" The officer's concern was showing in his eyes now.

"Yes, he sure has, but I hadn't known who it was that was doing it until now. I just caught him the other week at that abandoned house over there masturbating outside."

"You saw him masturbating?"

"Yes sir. He was on the back steps over there," I turned and pointed behind me to Terry's house before finishing, "and I had just pulled up in my backyard when I saw him over there doing that."

"Okay. Do you know if he's home now? I want to have a talk with Mr. Jerome."

"No, he's not anymore. When I went over there and asked if it was him that was doing it, he said 'No,' but when I told him I'd called the police because somebody saw him near my mailbox, he got mad. Next thing I knew, my friend Cherise—she's in the house—and I saw him come out of his house after he'd changed his jacket and put on a baseball cap. Then he jumped on his moped and went in the same direction you came. Did you see a little man on a red and black moped?"

"No, ma'am."

There was that heaviness again, tugging even harder at me. Was this really happening? Was this pervert really about to escape to freedom—on a get-away moped?

"Ma'am, what does Jerome look like?"

At least the officer was trying to get good information for the police report I'd have to go and later pick up. They always gave me their card and wrote the report number on the back of it. I still hadn't picked up the last report I put in, but since I knew it would always be on file I wasn't rushing to get it.

"He's a short, dark-skinned, older guy with low-cut hair—like a fade, or whatever it's called."

A car was slowly creeping by with another nosey person staring all in our faces, trying to see what was going on. As I looked back at the car as it was heading to the right towards the "Stop" sign at the other end of my road, I glimpsed what looked like a small figure on a moped.

The person was stopped at the side of Willow Creek Road, which was perpendicular to McNair Road. And he looked like he was trying to hide behind the bushes by the road.

"Wait a minute. Hey, do you see that?" I pointed at the man who was sitting there staring back at us from across the short distance. "Oh my gosh! That's Jerome! He must've circled the block!"

"Where?" The officer was looking too.

"See!" I pointed at the little man on the moped who must've thought we wouldn't see him because of the trees and small bushes in the yard right beside the road.

"That's him? He's sitting there watching us!" The officer was now on alert.

"Oh my gosh! Yes, that's him!" Wow. This pervert had to have been watching us the whole time. Apparently, when he took off to the left on the moped, he had only made a circle around the block so he could see when the police arrived to look for him.

"I'll be back. I think I can get Mr. Jerome to tell me what's going on."

And with that, the officer hopped back into his car, turned the blue lights on, and sped off towards the stop sign, making a quick left onto Willow Creek Road.

10

A Moped and a Charger

I could not believe what was happening right before my enlarged eyes. Realizing that the officer was headed in his direction, Jerome quickly—or as quickly as was possible on a moped anyway—did a perfect 3-point turn in the moped and headed back in the opposite direction down the road, past the house, and finally completely out of my viewpoint.

The officer must've realized he was running too because I could hear the rev of his engine in the distance as he sped up even more to chase him. There was no way that that moped could beat that Charger. Was there?

I didn't know if I should hop in the BMW and follow the chase too the way I'd always begged Mommy to do when I was growing up and had seen the cops speed by.

Or should I just wait in the yard?

I turned and looked over my right shoulder towards my screen door where Cherise now stood.

When she caught my eye, she opened the door. "The cop's gone?"

"Cherise," I turned and headed toward the steps of the porch, "you are not gonna believe this! My neighbor is trying to run from the police...on his moped!"

"*What?* What do you mean, 'He's trying to run from the police'? Dawn, you cannot be serious right now."

"Yes, Cherise!" This was the craziest thing I'd ever witnessed, let alone, ever experienced.

"But, on what though? Not that moped! Hump!" With her mouth gaped open in disbelief, Cherise pushed the screen door enough for me to slide through it.

"Yes, Girl. Remember when we saw him get on the moped and leave a few minutes ago?"

"Yeah..."

"Well, he must've turned and went all the way around the block because he was over there the whole time." I pointed in the direction of the bushes and trees. I continued, "Jerome was watching me and the cop talking, and when I spotted him and pointed to show the cop, he saw us and then he took off on the durn moped. The officer's gone after him in his Charger."

I let out a slight chuckle at the thought of Jerome hunched over the bars of the moped again like a real biker, thinking he's about to zoom away from the Charger before pressing the gas pedal as far as it will go and only to find that thirty-five miles an hour is its maximum speed. What a sight! That stuff only happened on movies, not in real life. But then again, I don't recall having ever seen a movie that featured a criminal trying to outrun the police on a moped either.

"Wow. Are you kidding me? Now that is ridiculous!"

"What do you think I should do now? Get in the car and follow behind them too?" I always asked Cherise for advice. I swear she always had the perfect, more levelheaded answers to any question I had.

"Dawn, no! You have to stay here and wait on the police to get back. You can't go chasing them both down too," she said with a slight laugh.

She was probably laughing at the mental image of tiny Jerome tooting along on the red and black moped being chased by the police officer in the green and white Charger while both being followed by a charcoal BMW with me behind the wheel in my huge hoop earrings and paparazzi-blocking sunglasses.

Now that was a crazy sight to even imagine.

"This is just so durn crazy." I headed across the room to where Cherise had now taken her usual spot back at the kitchen table. "Oh, I almost forgot to call Kevin back."

I hit the button on the side of my phone and waited for the screen to light up before entering my passcode and speed dialing him. After only one ring, Kevin answered, and I unloaded the new update. He sounded relieved that something was going to be done about the panty incidents, probably because it also meant that he wouldn't have to step outside of his character and confront anyone for messing with his wife.

Kevin reassured me that Jerome wasn't going to get away with anything this time, not with the police knowing who the suspect was. I sure hoped that was true. I had already begun pacing across the den again, constantly peaking out of the front door to see if the police officer was heading back towards my house from either direction, but he was nowhere in sight.

Cherise was on the phone with Brian now, and I could tell from the way that Kevin lingered on the phone that he didn't want me to hang up again. Probably not until the officer got back with a handcuffed Jerome.

As I walked back to the screen door and looked out for the last time, I couldn't believe what I saw passing the same set of bushes and trees across the field and headed down Willow Creek Road towards my road. There, I saw the oh-so-familiar-looking red and black moped slowly scooting along, my little neighbor directing it.

At the same time, the white and green Charger with the stern police officer at its wheel was following closely behind. It was like watching a lone ranger herding cattle slowly across a pasture. The officer had caught him and was bringing him back to justice!

Thank God!

But did this mean that now I had to get Jerome to tell the truth about what he'd done? And, on another note, why did the officer trust Jerome to drive himself back to our street anyway? I'd never seen anything like that happen before. What if he took off again as soon as they turned onto the road? Then what was I going to do?

"Boo," I almost forgot again that I still had Kevin on the phone. "Hey, I see the officer and Jerome coming down the road."

"Oh, good! I'm glad he got him! He's dumb as hell for trying to run on a moped."

"Yes! Thank God! But what if he lies again like he didn't do it?"

"Well, didn't you say Melissa saw him by our mailbox?"

"Oh yeah, she did, but she's still not home yet. She said she'll come over in a few."

"Well, don't worry then. It's going to be all right regardless." Kevin's words were always calming.

"Okay, Boo. I'll try not to worry. I love you."

"I love you too..." It was obvious that Kevin still didn't want to hang up.

I understood. I'm the same way when it's about him. I even hate it when he goes to the store at night. I'm the woman, but I always want to be by his side, protecting him too.

When the moped and the Charger made the right turn onto McNair Road, I opened the door and stepped back onto the porch with my cell still up to my face. Were they going to pull into my yard, which they'd reach first, or were they headed on past my panty-infested mailbox to Jerome's yard instead?

They did the former of the two.

"Boo, I'll have to call you back. They're outside pulling into our yard."

"Okay, let me know what happens."

"Okay, I sure will. Bye." I finally got off the phone but kept it in my hand as I stepped down off of the porch and waited on the officer to get out the car.

It was so strange to have Jerome sitting on his moped all of ten feet away from me. I crossed my arms, looking my lying neighbor straight in his eyes. To my surprise, the little man had dried tearstains flowing from the outer edges of his eyes to halfway down his cheeks.

A guilty man's tears often meant that he'd just made himself cry for the pity of another person. That person was usually a fed-up woman or a pissed-off judge.

Well, I wasn't falling for it. I was hoping the police officer wasn't falling for it either.

The officer got out of the car and walked over to me. "Well, ma'am, your neighbor Jerome here has something he wants to say to you. Jerome, get on off the moped."

"Yes sir." A regretful look swept across Jerome's face as he followed the officer's instructions and stood by the moped.

"I'm listening." I could feel my heart begin to race as I looked into Jerome's eyes, waiting on him to lie or, even worse, waiting on him to apologize like a child for me to then forgive him and say, "Oh, it's okay."

That was going to be some bull if it happened, and I wasn't having that either, so I impatiently waited.

"Okay now, Jerome. Tell this nice lady what you did."

The officer was really speaking to this grown behind man as if he were super slow to understand what he was saying. It was as if Jerome were a little infant who had to have even the easiest of sentences and words broken down to him in plain English.

Whichever the case, Jerome simply hung his head and looked down at the ground, saying nothing.

At that moment my patience must've fled the scene. Fed up, I spoke instead, directing my question to the officer. "Did he tell you that he put the panties in my mailbox?"

"Yes, ma'am. Jerome did tell me that he was the one who put

them there. Didn't you, Jerome?" The officer turned back to stare at Jerome, who looked up at him before responding.

"Yes sir, I did. But I didn't know no better."

I couldn't believe he was really gonna play this game with me. "What do you mean, you 'didn't know no better'?"

I cut my eyes into Jerome's as he looked back at me as if he wanted to say something else but wouldn't. This was the same rude jerk that had just cursed and made slick comments when I'd turned to go back to my house. This man had plenty of sense then and now, regardless of how innocent he was pretending to be. I wasn't falling for it. I wanted him to feel it and believe it deep down in his sick little heart.

The thud of my own heart was more like a bang as I began to wonder how it would all end. But true faith meant believing that God wouldn't fail me; he'd never failed me before when I needed him. Now I needed him more than ever because I was ready for it to all be over.

It would have to end today.

I calmed for a slight moment when I heard the officer tell Jerome to get the panties out of my mailbox. I'd already decided that I wasn't touching them anyway, and I'm sure Kevin didn't want to have to do it again, so the idea of Jerome retrieving his own stuff made it a little better.

What about taking the panties in as evidence and running them for DNA samples? They really looked like they could've belonged to a child, especially because of the multiple colors, including pink, which the whole world knows is a girly favorite.

It seemed as though the officer wasn't seeing things the way that I was.

At the same time, I did wonder if this meant that Jerome was about to get off that easily. Would he be ordered to retrieve the panties from my mailbox after apologizing like a little boy who'd just been scolded for wrongdoing and then merrily march home to his backyard to harass me yet another day?

I hoped and prayed that wouldn't be the case, but the first order had just been made.

In disbelief, I just stood there watching it all happen, waiting to see what the officer would do before I decided how to react. I could see myself getting right back on the phone after the officer had left so I could call Kevin and tell him the outcome: that the sicko had gotten away with only a slap on the hand. I could also see myself harassing him right back though. Petty, but maybe seeing how it feels would work.

No, I could not and would not stoop that low.

Heck no.

Just like a child who'd been caught red-handed, Jerome nodded his head in agreement with the officer's orders and said, "Yes sir." Together they walked to my mailbox so that Jerome could do just as he was told.

It was so strange to see him swiftly snatch out the panties as if he didn't want anyone to see what he was grabbing. He balled them into his right hand and smoothly slid his hand into his pants pocket and then removed the emptied hand.

It was just plain disgusting.

11

Dried Tears

Lord, don't tell me this man is gonna apologize and try to get away with this. I was hoping this officer would know better than to let Jerome do something so sick and then fall for his lies about it. Weren't police officers trained to recognize a lie?

All of a sudden, the officer and Jerome looked past me towards Melissa's house. I also turned my head to the left and looked to find Melissa walking toward us. Thank God!

As Melissa got closer to us I turned to address the officer. "That's my neighbor Melissa—the one who saw Jerome near my mailbox this morning."

"Hello, ma'am." The officer seemed to perk up a bit to this.

"Hey y'all." Melissa was always so pleasant.

"Hey, Melissa." I hugged my neighbor in relief, thankful that she made it before the officer left. "Thank you for coming. Jerome told the officer that it was him who put the panties in my mailbox."

Melissa turned from the officer to directly speak to Jerome. I bet he'd been the one stealing the UPS shipments from her doorsteps around Christmas the other year. Besides, he was always in his yard watching everything going on in the neighborhood. Heck, if it wasn't him, I guarantee he knew who the real culprit was.

"Now, Jerome, don't you know you can't be going in people's mailboxes putting stuff in them like that? Don't you know you can go to jail?" Melissa, too, was talking to this grown, sneaky behind man as if he didn't know any better. She should've heard him earlier when I'd confronted him.

Did he have her fooled too?

"Oh, um, yes ma'am. That's what he just told me; he said that I can't be doing that...nope."

This sick bastard!

If my piercing pupils could have burned straight through Jerome's lying ones, his would be burnt to a crisp. It was hard to believe that he really was playing this "I didn't know no better" game for them and even harder to believe that they might be falling for it.

"That's right ma'am." The officer was the first to speak again. "Jerome, why don't you also tell your neighbor what else you told me?"

"What else?" I looked from the officer to Tiny Tim. *Lord knows I didn't need any more. What else could this sicko have possibly done?*

"Go ahead and tell her, Jerome."

I was tired of these back and forth games that reminded me of kindergarten. Therefore, I was relieved when the officer finally gave up and told me what was really going on since Jerome wanted to act innocent and ignorant.

"Ma'am, Jerome here admitted to me that he was a peeping Tom. He said he went to jail for it years ago, but claims he doesn't do it anymore."

Wow...now I was not expecting to hear anything like that. Could it be possible that Jerome was the neighbor from across the street that the cousin around the corner had warned me about days after we'd moved into our house in 2009?

I thought I'd never forget that day.

***

When we first moved into the little blue house on McNair Road, it was sort of weird. Each time a car passed by the busy road, its driver would honk the horn as if he or she knew us. At first, I'd ask Kevin if he knew who it was, and his answer would always be "no."

After a few times of him asking me the exact question and me giving him the same response, we finally realized that the honking of the horn was the way that the neighbors said "hello" without formally introducing themselves.

In the beginning, living on McNair Road with people riding by bonking at us was just like it was growing up in Dillon. The small, white stone house that we moved to in 1990 was on the corner of Highway 9 and Cypress Street. Highway 9 was one of the main roads travelled by anyone in Dillon who either wanted to head to North Carolina or to the rural areas of the town, such as Oakland or Little Rock. Therefore, it stayed busy.

For as far back as I can remember we always sat on the long, rectangular porch playing "My Car-Your Car" or waiting and watching for relatives or family friends to ride by during their usual routes home. They always pressed hard on their horns to say "hello." Many often saw us on the porch, bonked their horns, and then circled right around the block to come visit with us. We looked forward to it, and it happened almost every day.

But that's the difference between the passersby in Dillon and those in Florence: I knew each of the ones in Dillon who bonked "hello" to us. Those bonking at Kevin and me years later were total strangers. Having strangers—although they were neighbors—

ride by and honk to speak still made us feel so welcome to the neighborhood. It was easy to feel right at home again.

Well, that was until one Monday after we'd officially moved all of our belongings in. That afternoon, I was on my couch watching TV after a tiresome morning of arranging clothes in each closet. I'd taken the day off to get the house in order while Kevin worked and the boys went to school and daycare. I don't even remember falling asleep, but a loud banging on the front door is what awakened me from a dream I'd fallen into.

I couldn't see very clearly through the scratched glass of the peephole, so I looked through the closed blinds of the window beside the front door. Parked in the yard was a blue Dodge truck with the driver's side door open, and a tall, dark-skinned man with cornrows and a white wife beater was standing at the door, waiting on an answer.

"Hey, how you doin'?" I said, as I opened up the wooden door, which was still blocked by a locked screen door. I wasn't unlocking it without having my Beretta with me, but it was in the bedroom. It was broad daylight, so it seemed okay.

"Hey, I'm good. How you? I live around the corner in one of the houses on the right," he said, and pointed to the left of him towards the set of houses off in the distance. "I saw y'all movin' in the other day, and I came to warn y'all about my cousin from across the street. He's a peeping Tom. He peeps at women, and he done had the cops called on him and everythang."

I stood there for a second, shocked and confused, yet very alarmed at what he was telling me, especially because it was his own cousin. "Oh my goodness," was all I could get out at first as he continued to speak.

"One girl even asked to use my phone to call the police on him 'cause she saw him peepin' in her window, and I sho' let her too. And that's my cousin!" he exclaimed.

"Wow, which house are you talkin' about?" This was all I could think to say at the moment.

"That one, right there," he said, and pointed to the white, stone house across the street that had two elderly men sitting on the porch, curiously watching while we spoke. "I just wanted to let y'all know," were the man's last words as I thanked him for warning me, and he hopped back in the truck and left.

I didn't even catch his name.

After years of seeing men across the street at the white, stone house and no "peeping" eyes, I'd completely forgotten about the idea of a peeping Tom being my neighbor.

***

To be living through the harassment years later and finding that my moped-driving neighbor Jerome was the one person who'd remained in that white stone house for all those years shook me from the inside out.

"Now Jerome, I can have you arrested for failing to stop for blue lights, for sexual harassment, and for indecent exposure. Your neighbor also told me about the incident of you masturbating on the back steps next door. You know, you can go to jail today." The officer's voice brought me back out of my own head.

"That's right, Jerome." Melissa seconded the officer's notion.

"I know…I understand now; that's what he told me." Jerome was still playing the same game.

Well, I wasn't having it.

"Oh, you knew what you were doing! This has been going on for months now! And I filed a police report the last time it happened too!" I finally found my voice and took advantage of it.

"Can I see your report, ma'am?" The officer seemed to perk up again and then took a step closer to Jerome.

"Yes, you sure can. I have the report number. I'll go get it from out of my wallet. I just want him to stay away from my mailbox…and me, especially since he's a peeping Tom."

"Yes, ma'am. Come here, Jerome." The officer gently guided Jerome's uncuffed right arm to steer his body toward the hood of the Charger. "Stay right here. Don't you move. Do you understand?"

"Yes sir." Jerome was being so obedient with those crusty tearstains on his face.

At that moment, I glimpsed a look of regretful innocence

sweep over him, and it made me rethink things. Did I want this man to go to jail for what he'd done to me? Was it supposed to have just been a joke? I didn't want to be responsible for sending anyone to jail.

On the other had, when it had been just the two of us minutes before, his true colors and aggression had flashed in a spurt of anger, and he'd been cursing. The way he was acting now had to just be for show and to be manipulative in order to get out of this. I couldn't fall for it.

After Jerome was situated, I turned and quickly jogged into the house and grabbed my wallet from the table by the front door. When I went back outside, I found the police officer on his cell phone with his supervisor. Maybe they were going to take this seriously.

Maybe Jerome would too and would finally leave me alone.

12

The Voice Outside

Everything that happened next seemed to zip by so quickly. When the officer hung up with his supervisor, he walked back over to Jerome, who hadn't moved from the front of the Charger, and told him to turn around. He then handcuffed him and advised him that because this wasn't the first report and because he admitted to putting the panties in my mailbox, he was under arrest for harassment.

Jerome's chin immediately flapped to the top of his chest like a five-year-old boy caught stealing the last chocolate chip cookie from the clear cookie jar.

I still couldn't fall for it. My boys tried those tricks all the time, just to get away with doing things they knew better than to do.

My boys!

I unlocked my cell phone and looked at the time. The school bus would be arriving soon and would be full of not only my own curious sons but also packed to capacity with screaming, playful children from all around the neighborhood. It was time for everyone to get out of my yard before that bus pulled up. I'd surely have a billion questions to answer, and the whole neighborhood would surely know all of my business.

The officer advised me that the investigator assigned to the case would soon contact me. The last officer had told me that too, but I'd never heard anything else...

"Jerome, who's around here that can come get you moped and take it inside your house?" The officer's voice always brought me back.

"Um, my uncle or my aunt."

"Where do they stay at?"

"Oh, down there in that brick house." Jerome nodded his head in the direction of the brick house to the left of Melissa's.

I had no idea that the older couple was related to him, but it made sense. I had, in fact, seen the lady taking pots, probably of Sunday's dinner, to Jerome's house around the time the old man who'd lived with him had apparently been sick.

"Okay. Tell me your uncle's phone number, and I'll let you call him and ask him to come down here to put your moped up for you."

Good. I needed that thing out of my yard before the school bus arrived.

"This is just crazy." I turned and looked at Melissa who hadn't left my side.

"Yeah, Girl, but Jerome knows better than that."

"I know he does, and I'm so glad you saw him today because I still wouldn't have known who was doing it if you hadn't seen him." I was so thankful it might finally be over.

After about five minutes, Jerome's uncle slowly pulled into the yard in his shiny, black Cadillac.

"Hey, how's everybody doin'?" he walked over to where we were still standing in my front yard. "So who's he been harassing?"

"Me." His question took me by surprise. I almost raised my hand...

I mean, was I not capable of being harassed by his sick nephew? And why be so nonchalant about it? Was this the everyday thing that Jerome was known for doing?

"Oh, okay. Jerome has some mental problems. We used to have to take him to talk to somebody about it."

I knew it! I knew someone was going to try to play that game again! Mental problems, my tail. He knew exactly what he was doing.

"But he's put panties in my mailbox a few times, and he's always in his yard watching me when I open my mailbox and find them.

"Yes sir," the officer spoke up again, "Jerome admitted that he's been harassing Mrs. Goodwin by putting panties in her mailbox. He's under arrest, and I'm taking him to the county jail. He'll have a hearing in the morning, if you or somebody in his family wants to go up there. Can you get his moped in his house and lock it up for him?"

"Oh, yes sir." At least the uncle was polite and didn't push the subject of mental illness any further.

"Sir, after he gets out do you think you and somebody in his family can see about getting him back to speaking to someone about his problems? I don't know yet what the investigator is going to do when she gets his case, but he needs to see somebody about this problem he's having again. These men ain't gonna let him keep harassing their women and gettin' away with it."

I agreed. Thank God, Kevin wasn't at home. I'd never seen nor heard of him fighting anyone ever in his life, but I still didn't know what he would've done to this little punk. Heck, if the tables were turned and a female was harassing my husband, I'd probably be squatting over a nasty prison toilet right now.

It was weird seeing the officer guide Jerome into the backseat of the Charger while Melissa and I, as well as everyone from the surrounding neighborhoods who kept circling the block, watched it happen right before our eyes.

Yet, it soothed my soul to know that it might be over.

Hopefully.

Prayerfully.

Thank God, I no longer had to wonder about anyone who might have been crushing on my husband. Thank God, I no longer had to wonder if the sweet girls whose children I loved for my own were crushing on him and trying to make me think that he was stepping out on me. And thank God, I no longer had to wonder if my boo, my strength, my man, and my confidant wasn't telling me about a female who was trying to get me angry enough to leave him.

Now I knew that my moped-driving neighbor Jerome was the one behind it all. Although I still didn't know why he was doing it to me, at least I could be confident that it was over.

***

When I heard the sweet voice of the investigator, I was quite surprised. I would've imagined a strict, deep-voiced male police officer on the other line, but it was a female. The pleasant investigator advised me that the county's victim's advocate representative would be contacting me soon to inform me about resources available to victims of crime in the area.

"Victims." That word didn't even sound right as an adjective being used to describe me. Not Dawn, a girl born and bred in Dillon, the place where you're taught how to defend yourself almost from birth.

The friendly investigator also advised me that she would call me personally and would let me know when Jerome would be released on bond. His hearing would be the next morning at 9, but I didn't want to go. I really didn't want to see him again.

What if I did and then felt sorry when I saw his dried tears? What if I changed my mind and told the judge I was dropping the charges? What if he decided to start—

To my relief, the investigator said I didn't have to appear in court because she had everything she needed. She would call me and let me know if and when he'd be released.

This was the first time I'd heard of a case going like this. Lord knows, I was relieved though. Yet, I still figured he would be released from jail soon.

I even thought he would be out the same day that he got arrested. I'd seen it happen before. I grew up knowing bits and pieces of how the system worked in my hometown. People were convicted of crimes, and if the crimes supposedly committed weren't too serious, the suspect would pay a measly ten percent of the bail amount and would be released on bond in no time.

I was waiting. But while I was waiting, I was praying and so were my praying mama and fired-up sister who I'd finally told what was going on with me.

"God will stop him!! Let us stay prayed up. You are MOMMY'S child!!! God has HIS hands on all of us!!!" On the night before the bond hearing, Keisha's text messages were pouring through. Like she'd added, "God will do like HE'S ALWAYS done...keep us safe and covered by HIS BLOOD. HE'S got this!!"

Because of faith, I knew it was true. I couldn't let go of my belief in the power of God and his ability to take care of the situation and work things out for me.

***

When Kevin told me that he'd found out that Jerome's family lives all around us with the exception of the Hucks and Melissa and her family, I didn't know if Jerome's family would retaliate against me for having him arrested. So I decided to turn the camcorder back on and record anytime I was out of the viewpoint of my mailbox.

I was surprised that Jerome wasn't released from jail until days after his bond hearing. Yet, the timing of it did make sense if he was receiving some type of disability check. In that case, he would get his check on the third of the month, and a relative like his aunt or uncle would be waiting to cash it for him and would probably then pay his bond.

When I received the phone call from the victim's advocate

around the 3rd of March, I figured that that was exactly what the case was. By that time, I had decided to stop leaving the house so much during the day. I wanted to see everything going on in my neighborhood, especially near my mailbox and yard.

But this would mean that I couldn't put the time into the volunteer work that I had been doing. The project I had been working on with the domestic violence victims would have to be turned over to the group of college interns to be completed.

I had already put in the majority of the work on the project, and for some reason, the interns weren't putting in much, or any, effort on their end. I couldn't blame them much since they were, after all, in college.

On March 3rd I messaged the director of the facility to let her know that I wouldn't be able to continue. I didn't mention the incidents with my harasser but simply told her that I'd been tied up with schoolwork and my website but added that the majority of the work had been done already. Everything I said was true, but the personal incidents didn't need to be told.

I couldn't just stop leaving the house altogether though. Baseball season was underway again, and Bryant would be having practice several afternoons during the week. Afternoon practice meant that I had to take him to the field and then stay there the majority of the time since Kevin would still be at work. It would all keep my mind off of things most of the time, I hoped.

It didn't...

I wondered what else was at the back corner of Jerome's house. For one thing, I had no idea that he had a dog over there. Then, for the split seconds I had glanced over there throughout the years, on the few occasions I had been able to sneak in a look without it being obvious that I was looking, I thought I saw a long wooden box with roofing nailed to it.

The times I'd seen Jerome and all of the guys there around the box I wondered what they were up to. I hadn't heard any muffled screams coming from that direction or from anywhere in my neighborhood at all, so I assumed that they were just hanging out and socializing with one another.

Other times, they were standing around stopping all the passersby they knew. You could always tell when someone they knew rode by because all you would hear was, "Hey!" Next thing you knew, a car would be slowing to a stop to get in on a short conversation with one or all of the guys.

That's how it was in Dillon too. It comes from knowing or being related to a lot of people and being excited to see them. There's nothing wrong with that...

Each day after Jerome was locked up, no one could be seen hanging around in his yard, but I still kept the living room blinds open as usual and constantly looked through the small gaps to see any movement on the road in front of my house. I'd learned the hard way to be more aware of my surroundings, which was unfortunate because we lived in what was normally a peaceful neighborhood. Even with the negative incidents that sporadically occurred, it still couldn't be considered "the hood" or "the ghetto."

If it had been, we never would have lived there. The people in our neighborhood had probably been there for their whole lives, and just like any neighborhood, it had its issues.

For the most part, my neighborhood always felt like home, especially when the harassment wasn't going on.

***

On March 6, 2014 when I heard a man's voice outside, I took it upon myself to look out the front blinds to see what was going on. A short figure in a dark-colored jacket was walking on my side of the road and then stopped to turn his head around to talk to someone I couldn't see.

It was Jerome! Jerome was standing there in front of my living room window. Was he doing this on purpose? I felt myself shaking and another trimmer drifted through my body again. Why did he have to stop directly in front of my window?

I was looking right at him, and I am sure that he could see me too. For a split second, it was almost like we even made eye contact. Or was I imagining that? Even if my eyes were fooling me, there was one thing I could do that wouldn't fool me: record him.

I grabbed by cell phone and started taking pictures of him standing there in front of my window. Then I used my camera's video recorder to catch all of his remaining actions, just in case. Seconds later, almost as if he was prompted, he turned and continued on to his house.

Out of all the spots on the road to stand and talk to an invisible person, why had Jerome chosen to stand on my side of the road directly in view of my double-paned den window? I don't know what he was trying to pull, but I wasn't taking any chances with him.

I took it upon myself to call the investigator to ask what I should do. When I told her what happened, her advice was for me to get a restraining order against him, just in case he was trying to intimidate me before court.

I agreed.

13

The Report

Soon, I went to the magistrate's office thinking I was going to get a restraining order against Jerome. Growing up, I didn't recall hearing that there was a step-by-step process for getting one. I'd always hear adults say, "Oh, I'm going to the police to get a restraining order against her."

At the magistrate's office years later I was thinking there was nothing more to getting one than asking the police for one, having them write it up on paper, and then waiting on them to serve the person doing the harassing.

Boy, was I ever wrong!

When I got out of the car and walked up the wheelchair ramp to the front entrance, I was surprised that a guard stood up front to check for metals—knives and other weapons—and guns. Although I wasn't expecting to be searched, I'd still left my stun gun inside my pocketbook in the car.

I never carried pocketbooks into government buildings. I didn't want to slip up and have any metal causing an alarm to go off. And I didn't want to innocently be arrested and jailed for being ignorant. No metal fingernail file or forgotten stun gun of mine was going to be the reason for me ever losing my freedom.

I'd learned about government office building procedures after working for a finance company in an even smaller town. As the assistant manager, whenever I'd taken customers to court to file judgments against them for not paying us, the magistrate's office I'd gone to didn't have a metal detector or a police officer guarding the entrance. I would walk right into the building each time and wouldn't even have to say a word to the clerk seated behind the glass window.

The courtroom in that town was the same way. You could walk right inside, and I don't recall ever seeing neither a metal detector nor a police officer by the door. But because my manager had always said that cellphones and pocketbooks weren't allowed in court, I knew not to ever try and take one. My keys, the customer's folder, and an ink pen were all I'd take with me inside, just in case.

The Offender I Once Defended

I don't play around with my freedom.

Today was pretty much the same. I only had my car keys and a folder with my police reports in it. Kevin and I had already been to the prison to get hard copies of the reports printed. Before leaving we'd sat in the parking lot and checked to make sure that the officer had reported everything I told him and everything that had happened, including the masturbation incident.

From what I'd read, the only thing the officer left off was the traffic citation he'd warned Jerome that he "could have charged him with" for riding without a permit. What I've learned from growing up black and living in black neighborhoods is that any time an officer says what he "could have charged" a person with, it usually means that he won't be charging that person for that particular thing.

Regardless, all the important details in the most recent report were there, and in all caps it stated:

ON 02-27-2014 AT 1258 HOURS I, DEPUTY ODELL, RESPONDED TO A RESIDENCE IN REFERENCE TO SEXUAL HARASSMENT. WHEN I ARRIVED ON SCENE I, DEPUTY ODELL, MET WITH THE COMPLAINANT-VICTIM MS. DAWN GOODWIN. MS. GOODWIN ADVISED ME, DEPUTY ODELL, FOR THE PAST SEVERAL MONTHS SHE HAS BEEN GETTING HARASSED BY HER NEIGHBOR A JEROME GORDON...MS. GOODWIN ADVISED ME SHE WENT TO THE MAILBOX TODAY TO FIND A PAIR OF

PANTIES IN THE BOX... MS. GOODWIN ADVISED SEVERAL WEEKS AGO GORDON WAS AT A VACANT RESIDENCE BESIDE HER HOUSE AND HE WAS MASTURBATING...I, DEPUTY ODELL, NOTICED GORDON ON WILLOW CREEK ROAD RIDING A MOPED. WHEN GORDON SAW ME, DEPUTY ODELL, IN MS. GOODWIN'S YARD HE STOPPED AND HID BEHIND THE BUSHES AND WATCHED THEN FLED THE SCENE HEADING BACK THE DIRECTION HE CAME. I INITIATED A TRAFFIC STOP ON GORDON DUE TO HE WAS STOPPED IN ROADWAY IMPEDING TRAFFIC AND I WANTED TO ASK HIM ABOUT THIS INCIDENT. I GOT GORDON STOPPED. I, DEPUTY ODELL, ADVISED HIM I INITIATED A TRAFFIC STOP IN HIS MOPED DUE TO IMPEDING TRAFFIC AND SUSPICIOUS ACTIVITY WITH THE HIDING BEHIND A BUSH WHEN HE SAW ME, DEPUTY ODELL. I, DEPUTY ODELL, PERFORMED A TERRY FRISK ON GORDON AND ADVISED HIM OF HIS RIGHTS. I THEN ASKED HAS HE BEEN STALKING MS. GOODWIN AND HE ADVISED NO. I ASKED HIM DID HE PUT PANTIES IN HER MAILBOX AND HE HUNG HIS HEAD AND STATED YES. GORDON ADVISED ME HE USED TO BE A PEEPING TOM YEARS AGO BUT HE QUIT THAT. I, DEPUTY ODELL, DETAINED JEROME GORDON AND CALLED CSC INVESTIGATOR MS. FLOOD. SHE ADVISED ME WITH THE EVIDENCE AT HAND AND THERE HAS BEEN A PREVIOUS REPORT TO

PLACE GORDON UNDER ARREST AND TRANSPORT HIM TO FLORENCE COUNTY DETENTION CENTER WHERE SHE WOULD BEGIN HER INVESTIGATION AND SPEAK TO HIM.

According to the report, Jerome was 45 years old. His hardened face made him look a little older than that to me, like maybe 53, 54, or even 55.

On the front page of the report, the Evidence Description stated the officer had collected "gray panties with multi-colors." My own description would've been more accurately matching what the panties looked like to me: little girl's undies. I could never imagine a grown woman wearing those old-fashioned panties with pink and gray colors.

Nevertheless, I was about to use both reports to get a restraining order against my moped-driving, sneaky, sicko neighbor so he would be arrested and put in jail if he ever went near my mailbox again.

When I found the room the guard directed me to after I'd told him my reason for being there, a heavyset light-skinned lady greeted me. For a moment, I imagined myself working there for the county, sitting in one of the empty desks to her left or right.

At one point when I was an undergrad at Francis Marion, I'd thought I would have a career working within the government one day. I'd even majored in Political Science and interned at the City-

County Complex. But I'd also changed my mind and went after a faster career path after graduation: the finance world.

Big mistake.

Continuing to look around the tiny room and take in the atmosphere, I quickly changed my mind. There were absolutely no windows in the small, dark room. That could never be a good thing.

For one, the building itself was the place where many angry citizens of the city of Florence went to settle disputes. And for another, I hadn't noticed an easy escape route as I'd walked down that long hallway which was full of windowless rooms.

No, thank you.

The pleasant, light-skinned lady advised me that court for the restraining order would be on March 31, the day before court for the harassment incident, and she asked if I still wanted to schedule it.

I will never understand why people had made it sound so easy to get restraining orders. Fooled me. Growing up, that used to be "the thing" when someone felt as if another person had violated them. They wanted to take legal action against them after getting physical with them hadn't worked. It happened way too often.

I'd heard the stories of relatives or friends of the family getting into fights with others—usually females and usually over two-timing men. The way they stopped the flattening of the tires and the sugar in the car tanks was by getting the restraining order. Everyone's ears perked up when the words "I took a restraining order out on her" were uttered.

They never bragged about all of the steps they had to go through to get that restraining order. We knew about the original fistfights. We knew about the scratched up vehicles or flattened tires. We knew about the no-good man still going back and forth—the one who had a child by both women. And we knew about the "getting" of the restraining order as they had always phrased it.

But that was apparently only part of it. Where, then, was the full conversation about all of the real steps needed to get a restraining order against a person?

Thank God, I never waited for that conversation. I'd still be waiting.

Because I didn't know there was such a thing as court for a restraining order, I needed more information on what would happen and if I needed the order and if it would really protect me from Jerome's watchful eyes and slick hands.

The woman advised me that I could go down the hall and actually speak with a judge to find out how the cases normally went.

I was pleasantly surprised to see a gray-haired black man seated behind the judge's chair in the large office. I didn't know any judges in the town, but it was good to see a black male in a position of distinction.

I respected how unbiased the judge was. He didn't have an emotional reaction at all when he told me how court would go. He only looked a bit disgusted when he read my police reports and discovered the manner in which Jerome had been harassing me.

He advised me that if my neighbor was found guilty on the day before court for the restraining order, then an order of protection would be put in place that would last forever which was way longer than the restraining order, which would eventually expire. I think he said that a restraining order would only last for about a year.

With that information, I decided to simply wait on my court hearing that would be in a couple of weeks. I had my police reports. I had Jerome's guilty plea, unless he tried to switch it on our court date, which I didn't even know was possible. I had witnesses to him admitting to harassing me, including the officer and Melissa. On top of all of that, the investigator had the prior case information from when he had been found guilty of being a peeping Tom.

All of that should've been enough for me to win in court and get the protective order I needed to stop the harassment once and for all. Maybe it was what Jerome needed after all these years. Maybe legal action instead of physical violence against him was all that was needed to scare him straight.

14
To Set a Fire

After discovering Jerome was the person harassing me, I'd also spoken with the Hucks about the situation and discovered that panties had been missing from their clothesline a few times. The mom and one of the daughters said that maybe Jerome had stolen them and put them in my mailbox.

That could've been true.

I clearly remember looking out my window one morning months back and seeing Jerome in the field across from my house. Mr. Nosey was looking in the direction of the Hucks' house. For all I know now, he could've been in that spot, checking to see if anyone was at home before making his move for some panties.

I hadn't been seeing Jerome at all for the majority of March. That was, until the day of the fire.

It was March 28th and I was still at home, unemployed but doing what felt like a billion different tasks...life always has to keep moving when you're serious about doing better and having better.

For days, I had been noticing people coming and going next door at Terry's abandoned house. I assumed they were all somehow related to him. If they weren't related to the family, I'm sure Terry's aunt, who lives in the brick house to the right of his, would've quickly gotten them off the property.

Did I mention I later found that Terry's family is also Jerome's family too?

When I got up that morning, I opened my blinds so the radiant sunlight could flood through, brighten, and naturally warm my house. The thin tree limbs outside were swiftly swaying in the breeze. I could only imagine how good it felt them. It was such a quiet, peaceful morning, so I went about my day before the bus with my lively boys was set to arrive.

When Bryant and Lil' Kevin got home that afternoon, it was their usual snack time as they were always starving by the time the school day was over. After giving them their snacks, I looked out of the blinds that faced Terry's house and noticed a different guy over there, one I'd never seen before, in the yard between Terry's house and his aunt's. He didn't appear to be doing anything sneaky and was simply burning something—probably clothes or trash, is what I assumed.

I couldn't tell from the distance, but it was a bit strange that someone would be at Terry's house burning stuff when he had been gone for so long that nothing should've needed to be burned.

Honestly, when I see a young person—like the one I was staring at from my window—burning something outside, for a moment I think back to the suspenseful movies I'd seen where criminals would be trying to burn bloody clothes or other evidence after committing heinous crimes.

Hopefully, that's not what the young man next door was doing.

It was becoming so windy outside that the fire was rippling while the young man fanned it with what looked like a metal rectangular slab. At that point, I couldn't tell if he was trying to put it out or if he was trying to keep it going. Regardless of which of the two he was trying to do, the fire began to get a bit out of control.

Every few minutes, I looked back out the window to check the new status of the fire. It was still burning and being fanned by a nameless stranger. The last time I looked, I saw that two more guys had joined him. One of them was Jerome.

This time, Jerome wasn't at the back steps of Terry's house masturbating in a trance-like state. And this time, Jerome wasn't sneaking to my mailbox to drop off panties to later watch my reaction as I discovered them. This time, Jerome was also fanning the uncontrolled fire.

Idiots.

That's the only word that could accurately describe the grown men out there doing something so stupid. Out of all the days that had passed that I hadn't felt a single gust of wind, this young man had chosen today—the windiest day in months—to burn a fire, in someone else's yard! Were they even considering what would or could happen if the fire got out of control?

Apparently not, because the last time I walked to the window for an update, the fire was already spreading across Terry's yard.

Lord knows I didn't want that fire to cross the dirt road and spread to my yard too, if that was even possible. I didn't know, so I was concerned. At that moment, the only thing I knew to do was pray that they put the fire out before it spread any further.

I couldn't be the one to call 911 again. Everyone would know I'd done it. Me: the now fearful woman standing by her kitchen window every few minutes to see what the guys were up to. Me: the same woman with the scowl on her face as she looked outside in disgust. The same woman who'd had Jerome arrested for harassment.

Jerome and his crew seemed way too unbothered by the fire. I would've been panicking, but they were fanning almost like a queen would as she sat on her golden throne.

I just didn't get it.

"Look, Mama, the bushes are on fire!" Lil' Kevin and Bryant were by the double windows as soon as they realized what was going on.

It seemed as if everyone was panicking except the people who should have been panicking.

"I know, Baby. Only idiots burn fires on dry, windy days. Let's just pray that they get it put out, okay?"

"Yes ma'am!" Kevin and Bryant responded in unison. My boys knew all about prayer too.

"But, Mom, they don't have any water!" A bright-eyed Bryant couldn't take his eyes away from the men or the slowly spreading fire that was now scorching the bushes next to Terry's house.

"I see that, Baby. Hopefully, someone's called the fire department by now. All those cars are slowly riding by and watching too, so I hope somebody's called and said *something*. In a minute, I'm gonna call my durn self because I can't have that fire hopping over the road and hitting our grass and house too."

We waited, prayed, and watched for another five minutes to see if the guys would get the fire out. When the fire spread to the front of Terry's yard and began to torch the tallest bush that was next to the light pole by the dirt road, I finally called 911.

Enough was more than enough.

After calling 911 and telling the operator "the idiots at the abandoned house next door had lost control over the fire they were burning," this time, she said she was immediately sending help.

Feeling a slight sense of relief, I returned to my kitchen window, asking God to please not let that fire spread to our house.

Within minutes, the first truck from the local fire department was on the dirt road next to our house, and one of the firefighters was suiting up to go fight the spreading blaze.

My boys were in such amazement—mouths and eyes both widened as far as they could extend—at seeing the firefighters coming to everyone's rescue, that they began jumping and cheering.

I could see Jerome out there in Terry's yard with the other guys, now heading closer to my front yard as the other firefighters took on the task of putting out the remaining sparks that had already eaten away the majority of the now blackened, crispy yard. But did the other guys outside watching the firefighters successfully kill the flames know what Jerome had done to me? They had to. Seems like the whole neighborhood knew but simply refrained from acknowledging it, with the exception of the guy driving the blue truck, the Hucks from the dirt road beside us, and Melissa.

It was the same "hear no evil, see no evil" scenario that was still plaguing the black community, in just a different decade. It was the way it had probably always been.

People need to speak out about the harmful behaviors done by even the closest of relatives and family friends. The harmful behaviors that too many of us fail to acknowledge, stand up against, or try to prevent from happening...

The day of the fire was the last I'd seen of Jerome until our court appearance on the first of April.

15

I Will Trust

The night before court had been rough. My brain was too flooded with thoughts that blocked me from having a good night of rest. I constantly imagined what Jerome and his family would have to say the next day.

Jerome had already confessed to the police officer that had arrested him on the day of the last panty incident. The investigator had already told me that Jerome had the old conviction on his record for being a peeping Tom. I had the hard copies of my police reports from when I'd reported finding the panties in my mailbox.

All the evidence seemed to be there, but was it enough to find Jerome guilty the next day? And what if he tried to use his mental state as an excuse for harassing me? Then, what would happen?

That excuse had gotten criminals out of trouble in the past, even murderers. Jerome hadn't murdered anyone, as far as I knew, so harassing me because of a mental disorder shouldn't even be a good comparison.

Was I screwed?

I flipped back and forth throughout the night, cuddling in closer and closer to Kevin to the point in which he was getting pushed closer and closer to the edge of the bed. I needed him...

I didn't want to go to court the next morning, yet I didn't want Jerome to automatically have his charges dropped by default if I didn't show up. I needed for Jerome to be stopped. If I didn't do anything, there was a strong possibility that he would just lay low for a while and later begin harassing the next woman he'd peeped out.

***

"Boo, I really don't wanna go." I walked into the den where Kevin had prepared coffee for us and was waiting on me to join him.

"Why not? You know you need to be there." His words were gentle but serious as he, too, knew how the process usually goes when you accuse someone of a crime and don't show up to court.

"I know…" I sat down in the loveseat across from him and started sipping on my coffee, my hand shaking a little as I tried to avoid spilling the steamy drink on myself.

"I mean, so what do you wanna do?" Kevin leaned in closer to look in my eyes before adding, "You know, ultimately it's your decision, but I still think you should be there."

He sat his favorite L.A. Lakers coffee mug down on the floor beside his foot then stood and came over to sit beside me on the loveseat.

"Look." He softly caressed my thigh before grabbing my hands into his own. "They're gonna find him guilty, and that's all there is to it. I'll be right there with you. You don't have anything to worry about. You have your copies of the police reports, and the lady already told you he was convicted years ago. All of that and his confession should be all we need."

Kevin's confidence always had a way of making me feel more confident, regardless of the situation.

"Okay, Boo. Thank you for that." I managed to muster up a slight smile in agreement. He was right, but I was still quivering inside.

"Come on, let's get ready." He softly patted me on my exposed thigh, stood up, and started towards the bedroom.

I followed.

I threw on the gray dress pants and blouse I'd ironed the night before and examined myself in the mirror before deciding to wear a blazer too. I smirked a little at my chocolaty reflection staring back at me. Well, at least I looked okay.

The ride to the courthouse was only twenty minutes away, but time constantly stood still, making it feel more like twenty hours away.

My head was so full of "what if?" and "why?" that all I wanted to do was go to sleep and not think about any of it ever again. Like, what if Jerome's aunt and uncle came to court today to speak on his behalf? What if the judge let Jerome slide because he, too, was fooled into believing that the peeping Tom "wasn't right in the head?" And why was this happening to me anyway?

This was too much for one person to have to think about.

I called Mommy and Keisha on the ride to the courthouse, asking them to please pray for me to calm down. I wasn't surprised to find that they'd already been praying too. I knew it was true. Anytime I needed an extra Word from God or a prayer, I knew the people to call.

"I will trust in the Lord..." No matter what age I am, I can still hear Mommy singing her praises to God while she was in the kitchen cooking us a hot, tasty breakfast with the window open. The fresh breezes of air always seemed to circulate the mouth-watering aromas, not only around the cozy room, but also throughout the entire house. Those were the good ole days.

Now, I just had to trust in the Lord myself. I had to trust that he would give me peace again. I had to trust that Jerome would be found guilty and would be ordered to stay away from me. I had to believe that God would make my enemies leave me alone if I asked and trusted in him.

   I was asking and trusting…

16

Not Today

I guess this is it. I slightly turned my head to the right of me to see what my stalker's response would be after I answered the judge. But he simply stood there still looking straight ahead with a fake, innocent look on his sweaty face.

With my four-inch heels on, I stood a few inches over Jerome. I could've smacked him right then and there, maybe knocking some sense into him the same way the men from the neighborhood had tried to do when they'd caught him watching their women.

But I didn't want to go to jail.

He was not worth me potentially ruining my life. I had a family to think about too. My actions or inactions would affect their lives as well as my own.

But it was really pissing me off how this pervert wanted to act as if he didn't know that putting panties in my mailbox was wrong. I don't care what his uncle said. This sick bastard knew what he was doing and would do it again if he were allowed to. That was his known history.

I hadn't forgotten how Jerome had reacted when I confronted him after discovering that he was my harasser. He'd pretty much bucked up when I was walking away. Today seeing him being humble and not mumbling a single word was upsetting, but I had to keep my outwardly calm composure.

I rolled my eyes away from the sight of him and tried to focus my thoughts. I doubt that any of the other women in the neighborhood who'd been harassed by Jerome had reported it to the police. At least I know one hadn't.

***

A few days after I'd filed the police report in February, the same guy from the neighborhood who'd originally warned me about the peeping Tom had seen Kevin in Dollar General and had decided to tell him about another incident.

"Hey, man, Jerome must've been botherin' your wife. I saw them out in the yard with the police the other day," he offered when Kevin looked at him, recognizing him as another neighbor from around the corner.

"Yep. Man, we found out it was him bothering her when I wasn't at home. He'd been puttin' stuff in our mailbox."

"See, I tried to tell y'all about him." The guy shook his head and continued, "Last year, a lady from a few houses down from mine caught him peeping in her window. She told her husband, and he beat the hell outta him. They ain't had no problems with him ever since."

When Kevin got home from the store that day and told me what happened, I could feel eyes on me all over again. Had Jerome been watching me at times when I hadn't known about it? Were there times when he was standing by our bedroom window in the darkness listening to Kevin and me make love or trying to peep inside at me?

I had to get those thoughts out of my head.

***

The warm Folgers coffee I'd sipped that morning was slowly boiling up inside of me, about to swell into my throat and explode all over that concrete courtroom floor. It was almost too much to handle and take in at once. I hadn't even wanted to see Jerome at all, but here we were.

This magistrate courtroom in Florence County was different. Off to the left side of the judge's bench were rows of seats filled with uniformed police officers and other important-looking people. A few were in regular clothing; I guess those were the undercover officers.

I'd thought the courtroom setup would be the same setup as the hearings I'd previously attended with two separate tables and chairs behind each, one for the defendant and the other for the plaintiff, all in front of the bench with the judge and his court recorder. In this courtroom, Jerome and I were not behind our own individual tables. We were standing in front of the judge's bench, a couple of feet apart from each other, separated only by the investigator.

I had been communicating with the investigator, who'd kept her word on keeping me updated about everything going on. Seeing her in person for the very first and last time was a bit weird. She looked the way she sounded over the phone—she was a beautiful, mild-toned blond who had concern behind her serious blue eyes.

I hadn't expected her to be standing there beside Jerome as if she were his psychologist. She seemed empathetic toward him, yet she still had an air of fairness and understanding about the situation as a whole, from both sides. Maybe she had determined that Jerome really was sick in the head.

I understood the reasoning behind it.

In Dillon, I'd heard the stories about how some people let men get by with committing crimes like this by giving them the excuse that "there's something wrong with them."

I've never been one of those people.

Yet, I was thankful for the investigator. She'd done everything she was supposed to do. She had investigated the case from the very beginning, and on the day Jerome was taken into custody, she was the one who advised me about his previous conviction. I guess she'd either known him personally or had known of him and his history. She'd even told me that she was going to try and get him registered as a sex offender since he'd admitted to harassing me and because he had the peeping Tom problem.

What I remembered the most about my court date was everything that was said after Jerome, the investigator, and I were all called to stand in front of the judge.

After the investigator went first to present the facts of our case and announced that Jerome was pleading guilty, the judge turned to Jerome for a response, which was nothing.

Next, the judge turned to look at me. "Ma'am, do you have anything that you want to say today?"

I thought for a second before ending with the only eight words that came to mind, the only words necessary: "I just want him to leave me alone."

That was it.

When the judge announced his ruling, I felt a release from

within that made me want to scream and shout across that courtroom—and I had never shouted before.

Jerome was found guilty of harassment. My sick neighbor was ordered to pay a fine and was then told the grounds of the order of protection: "Don't look at her. Do not go near Mrs. Goodwin's mailbox. If you see her on one side of the street, you'd better not even speak to her. Do you understand, Jerome?"

"Oh...yes sir." Jerome nodded his head in agreement like a scared slave who'd just been caught lusting after his master's wife.

"If you go near her or her mailbox, you will be locked up. Do you understand?"

"Yes sir!"

Thank you, Jesus! Lord, I thank you! Nobody but God turned this situation around. Nobody but God allowed things to play out the way that they had. Nobody but God brought me through it all.

Even when I felt that I'd lost, I'd won. My harasser had been uncovered and stopped. The problem with Jerome was over and hopefully there would be no more issues. I could move forward in life and get back focused on my future.

***

Then I had no time to pout or complain, let alone really get over the shock of what happened to me. It was as if things sped right back up. Kevin had to go back to work that same day. By that afternoon, I was following up with Lil' Kevin's teacher to make sure that his behavior was better after getting into a silly altercation with a former friend the day before. Then I had to be at home for the school bus that would be there by 2:25.

I was also searching again for a full-time job to help out around the house. Since my unemployment had run out, I wasn't receiving any real income other than the small jobs I did for my website, and I wouldn't have my master's degree and be able to start teaching until the next year. I had to do something.

But that wasn't it. My life has never been only about me and about my issues. It never should be. Not when you have a family. I had to be there to support my sister who'd been diagnosed with Multiple Sclerosis and would be in Florence that afternoon for an appointment.

When I arrived to the doctor's office, it was a relief to squeeze Mommy and Keisha and show them in person, instead of over the phone, that I was unharmed, at least physically anyway.

Mentally, on the other hand, it was time to let go of wondering if someone would go near my mailbox again. I had to make up in my mind that if someone did, then I'd just have to call the police again.

It was time. Time to let go of fear. Time to live

17

The Essay

It's amazing how you can write something one day and totally forget about it months later.

After being in court and still being out of work for a few months, I found myself struggling to go straight to sleep at night. Whenever my family finally went to bed, I spent most of my time focusing on schoolwork in the silence of the night and then watching reality TV to get my mind off of the tiresome day.

On one night a couple of months after Jerome's conviction, I opened up my laptop to search for a nonfiction essay or a poem to submit for publication on our school's website.

In Word, I began scrolling through the alphabetically arranged documents, looking for any titles that caught my eye. One of the first essays I came across was entitled "Accusations Aren't Convictions." I had last saved it in October of 2013. I opened the document and began reading the first sentences:

In 2009, my realtor Dennis had just shown us our current home. Two weeks later, Kevin had introduced himself to our neighbors in the surrounding houses, and we were excited to be moving in, but I had to check the South Carolina Law Enforcement Division (SLED) website for nearby sex offenders. I just wanted to make sure that there were none near my family.

I was glad to find that none were on my road.

As I read, I could vividly remember that I'd written the essay in one of my favorite nonfiction classes from a previous semester. It was for our literary journalism assignment, and I'd chosen to write about sex offenders—specifically, how for most of my life I'd heard about different guys being accused of being those types of criminals, but I'd also never heard anything about them actually being convicted of the accusations.

As I finished the first paragraph, I chuckled a bit. This was the essay I'd screwed up a little. I'd gotten so deep into the first draft that I'd discussed way too many different scenarios I'd heard through the years. I'd gone so far that my professor had asked me to narrow the essay down and develop only a smaller amount of the individual stories.

I'd traced back everything I could remember in that one essay, especially info about sex offenders I'd discovered in the area before we purchased the house in 2009.

When I read the next section, I gasped in horror at what I'd written. I'd begun to go into the story of the day that the man in the blue truck had awakened me to warn me about my neighbor from "across the street." Then the next paragraphs went into the description of the day that I'd gone back to work and had spoken about the incident:

While chatting with my manager and her best friend Sherrie, I revealed what the guy had told me that afternoon. Coincidentally, Sherrie said the story had to be true because she used to hang out at that house too.

She said, "One day, Junior had a house full of people there, and he was holding a baby boy and was molesting him when nobody was looking."

I was shocked. Sherrie wasn't saying anything about a man being a peeping Tom, but she was talking about a child molester, which was extremely disturbing.

After hearing about the supposed sex offender across the street, we've taken all types of precautionary measures. I've had an alarm system installed, and my husband purchased a guard dog that's so protective of us that it won't let our neighbors go to their mailboxes if it's untied. We posted "No Trespass" and "Beware of Dog" warnings all over the yard, along with the ADT alarm system stake in the front yard and ADT stickers on most of the windows.

It's been over four years that we've been living here, and I have yet to see peeping eyes from the direction of the white house. The other year, I stopped seeing either of the elderly men who were on the porch that day. I have, however, seen a middle-aged man and a teenage boy there, but I knew that the boy couldn't be the person Sherrie was referring to, simply because of his age. However, that still left the one other guy.

It was almost sickening to come across the section describing my neighbor—the once nameless, faceless person everyone but my husband and I seemed to know so much about:

Later I learned that his name was Jerome. He seemed like a nice guy, but I wondered if he was, in fact, the same man accused of molesting the baby boy. Sherrie had said that Junior dressed nicely and wore his shirts tucked in his pants. Jerome did too. His button-down, plaid shirts were always tucked into his pants, and from what I had seen, I didn't recall him ever walking around looking like a thug with white tees and baggy jeans. But were "Jerome" and "Junior" the same person?

The frightening part of it all was that my youngest son was so friendly that when he saw Jerome riding by on his moped, he'd yell out, "Hello, Neighbor!" and try to spark a conversation. To my relief, our neighbor never took the opportunities to engage in talk with Bryant, so the molestation accusations have been in the farthest corners of my mind.

I must admit, Jerome has been my ideal neighbor. He waves "hello" when he sees us, but he sticks to his own business and doesn't bother anyone.

Even so, after finding out his name, I did another SLED search and thankfully found nothing. I also checked scnow.com, which is the go-to website for all local news in South Carolina, but I found nothing.

The cousin's warnings and Sherrie's story both seemed so real, so they had to have some truth to them, right? Or maybe the person they were referring to moved away or is now locked away in jail...I don't know. It makes me wonder if the story from the cousin was true. If not, what was the man's motive for telling me? And, if Sherrie's story wasn't true, what was her motive for lying?

Those questions were unanswered then—at the end of October 2013, but not in April of 2014, a measly six months later. And my "ideal" neighbor? Jerome turned out to be more like my "ideal" nightmare.

Apparently, everything different people had said about him had been true. I really don't think "Jerome" and "Junior" were two different people. I think, or better yet, I am sure that Jerome is the same person who did those things to that baby.

Jerome may have hurt an innocent baby boy who couldn't speak up for himself, but I do thank God that the pervert failed at continuing to harass me. I was probably the match he never thought he'd ever get.

If he'd done the same thing to anyone else from Dillon, he wouldn't even be able to pry his eyes open to look at another female again, not after the beating he probably would've gotten.

I wasn't like everyone else though. I liked the idea of at least attempting to handle my problems legally. That way, I would keep myself out of trouble. Like I mentioned, jail and hell are two places I never want to visit.

Still, I couldn't believe it was me who was going through this. It was so unreal. Me? Harassed?

Never...

Tears flooded my eyes, making the computer screen blurry as if I were looking at a foggy mirror. It was like being trapped inside of a strange scene in a Lifetime movie, stuck inside of a main character's head as she discovers all of these horrible things that have secretly gone on around her...stuck inside of her head as she finally uncovers a truth that has been there all along.

I wiped my eyes and continued reading, searching for anything else I'd mentioned about my harasser:

Deep down, I had once been biased and believed that there must be some truth to rumors of sexual offense crimes, especially those against children, but the last SLED search showed me that there is a huge difference between an actual conviction and an accusation. Anyone can accuse someone else of violating his or her children, but when there is no actual conviction, then it's time to consider the fact that the accused just might be innocent.

"...just might be innocent."

Wow. I just wanted to run and wake up Kevin. I needed for him to shake me and wake me from this humiliating nightmare.

I felt stupid. To be going through the harassment and not piecing together the fact that the person who harassed me was the same faceless neighbor I had once defended made me want to erase every trace of the essay, hide away, and never talk about any of it again.

It was nauseating.

It was scary.

And I was totally mortified.

Forget the essay about accusations not being the same as convictions. That was before my eyes were accidentally, yet thankfully, pried open to the truth, the truth that my neighbor had harassed me. The truth that my neighbor was sick in the head. The truth that my neighbor was a peeping Tom...

My neighbor...

Jerome.

The same pervert who'd cunningly watched me for God knows how long...

I was the only person in my house who was awake, but I felt utterly embarrassed. How could I not have known that Jerome was the person? And why had I allowed myself to forget so much? Would people think that I'd known the whole time about Jerome putting panties in my mailbox, and I simply wanted to play victim and gain attention?

All alone in the quiet den, I cried myself to sleep that night. I would wait to talk to Kevin. I didn't want to disturb his peaceful sleeping with the nightmare I was experiencing while I was awake.

18

Shall I be Moved?

I think my unbothered outward demeanor each time I opened my mailbox and saw the panties had probably fueled Jerome and made him want to continue to harass me.

I admit, he was pretty clever. I guess he'd seen me each time I was at the window setting the old camcorder up on the desk so that it would accurately record my mailbox from that weird angle.

Looking back now, I'm also sure Jerome had seen me playing with the blinds, opening them more or less, as I tried to get the end of the camcorder perfectly arranged between the small opening.

Then I never thought about the fact that the camcorder has a red, very noticeable light that, if seen, would draw attention to the person seeing it as they wonder if a gun with a silencer and laser beam is being pointed at them. Kevin's the one who pointed that out to me.

I guess I just never would've thought that anyone around here would be watching me like that. It's been embarrassing, and I don't want the "well, why don't y'all move?" questions. And I don't need to hear the "well, you should've known" statements either.

I don't want to hear it. I don't need others' questions when I'm still sometimes questioning myself about how I didn't realize Jerome was my harasser. Like how didn't I realize that the nosey neighbor outside was watching my goings and comings and leaving his treat for me?

I still don't know why.

Maybe I never will.

But what I do know is that I can't question God or the bad things that happen in my life. I can't. I have to accept the fact that everything has happened for a greater reason. Getting laid off was a blessing for me. It was my chance to finally go back to school. Being harassed was a lesson. You should never be so involved in your day-to-day life that you are ignorant about what else is going on outside of the imaginary box that you've put yourself in.

***

Months later, I still found myself pinning open the curtains and watching my mailbox. Any time I heard the crunch of steady footsteps on the dirt road, I ran to my kitchen window blinds to see who it was. Any time I heard a male's voice trailing in the wind outside, I looked out the front window to see who it was.

It was no way to live.

In fear...

I don't know why I even felt that way. What were the real possibilities that the same pervert would harass the same person after his conviction? History, and rumors, had shown that Jerome moved on to the next person after he'd been dealt with, so why wouldn't he do the same with me?

There were times when I was riding down McNair Road and was about to turn into my driveway when I could still clearly hear the judge's words to Jerome all over again: "If you see her, you'd better not even look at her. You'd better not even speak to her."

I remember standing there in front of the judge that day. It was like I was there, but I wasn't. I was in a state of disbelief. No way was this happening to me in my real life. No way had I been harassed. No way had I not resulted to violence like people from back home would've quickly done. No way.

***

"We're at a point now where we gotta make a decision." Kevin took another pull of the bitter-smelling cigar and leaned back in the wooden bench beside me while we watched the rain pouring around us.

We loved sitting on the porch together and having serious discussions or small talk, or simply reflecting on life.

"What kind of decisions?" I already knew what he was referring to, but I asked anyway.

"About whether or not we're gonna stay here. Now we know that these guys, like Jerome and Lionel, got family all around us—hell, I think they're family too—and they ain't goin' nowhere. They probably been here their whole lives."

"Yep, you're right..."

He sat back up and took another pull from the cigar before it started to die out again. "We gotta decide if we wanna still stay here for the rest of our lives or not. You're at a point where you have your new career coming up soon, and we wanna buy a new house or add on to this one, so we need to decide what we're gonna do."

"Right…" I sat up and reached for his cigar and took a small pull. I had been thinking the same thing. It really was time to decide.

When you come from a lower income household and decide you want to have more as an adult, you don't make decisions based off of the "what ifs" of life. You don't wonder "what if my neighbor harasses me" when you decide that you want to buy a starter home that you can either renovate one day to create your dream house or that you can use as rental property after purchasing your dream house years later. Realistically, you also don't wonder: "What if I lose my good-paying job after accruing all of this debt that I need a job to get out of before I can get that dream house away from my sicko neighbor?"

I know I never thought about those things. No one expects to be harassed.

It's all about what you do when situations occur. Do you take physical action like everyone else does, or do you follow the rules of the law? Do you give up and go back to mama until your finances are straight enough to afford a new place after finding a new job, or do you stay where you are and be firm and determined until you find better?

"What do you think then? I'm going to leave it totally up to you because I'm okay either way. I love it here, and this is a good neighborhood, but I'm also willing to move if that's what you want to do. It's quiet around here, and I hardly see Jerome, but it's still up to you. I know you don't have anything else to worry about anymore."

"You really don't think so? I mean, I don't either. I know that no matter where you stay, every neighborhood has its problems. Crazy people are everywhere. Good thing is, the courts stopped Jerome. He can't even look at me, or he's going to prison. And I love it here too...so I don't wanna move."

That was it. Our decision was made. We weren't moving away but were staying in the same house, in the same neighborhood.

***

Well, that was until the day that Terry magically reappeared. I had been in the den watching TV when I heard a man's voice on what I thought was the dirt road beside the house. I stood up from my spot on the couch and quickly walked over to the kitchen window where the curtains were pinned open and the blinds were slightly ajar. Instead of twisting the rod to further open the blinds, I slid one open and peeked out.

It was Terry!

He was headed from his mailbox directly across the street from his house and was slowing down to talk to a guy in a passing car. I never thought I'd be so happy to see him return. I was so overjoyed that I called Kevin at work to tell him the news.

For a couple of days, Terry and some other guys spent most of the afternoon cleaning trash out of the house. I was excited about the idea of him getting the eyesore finally fixed. But after only about a week, the movement stopped, and Terry was gone again.

Another week passed, and there was a knock on our door at 11:30 at night, which was right after Kevin had come in from doing a store run. None of our relatives were in town, so we weren't expecting any guests.

"What the hell?" Kevin's usual friendly tone of voice was gone.

As he got up and walked over to the back door, I followed right behind. I was going to see who it was and would take charge of a situation if I needed to.

"Who is it?" When Kevin got to the backdoor, he got straight to the point.

"Lionel."

"Well, durn. He must've seen when you pulled up in the yard!" I knew how Lionel operated. I was just surprised that he actually came when he knew Kevin was at home.

Kevin looked at me in agreement then clicked the locks on the heavy door before furiously snatching it open. Only the thin glass screen door stood between nasty-looking Lionel and us. But this time, Lionel didn't look at me at all. He only looked at and spoke to Kevin.

"Yeah? Why you knockin' at my door, Lionel? Didn't I tell you to stay away from here?"

"Y-yes sir." Lionel quickly answered. "I-I wanted to see if you got some matches I could get so I can light my heater…I live next door at Terry's now."

Kevin and I locked eyes, thinking the same thing at the same time. Pressing my back against the wall beside the wooden door, I allowed my weakened knees to give way as I slowly slid to the floor.

Epilogue

On November 9th, 2015, I rushed to my English Composition class and began to write out the day's lessons on the blackboard. It was ten minutes before six. Class began at six, and as usual, only a couple of students had made it in from their first-shift jobs.

I'd just put my cell phone on vibrate after leaving the faculty workroom across the hall when it began to vibrate, causing it to slide down the slanted, wooden podium. I quickly snatched it before it could hit the carpet.

When I looked at the screen, I saw that it was Melissa. Melissa would have known that I was at work. It must've been important for her to be calling me. I don't think we've ever called each other just for small talk.

I picked up the Note 4 and swiped the phone to the right to answer, heading to the classroom door and towards the faculty workroom.

"I'll be right back." I looked over at the few students who'd made it to class before completely exiting the room.

"Hey, Melissa," I said as I heard my neighbor answer on the other line. "How you doin'?"

"Okay, is Kevin at home?" I just got to my house, and my door is wide open."

"Oh my goodness. Don't go inside of there! Kevin's not home, but he's on his way. I can call him and tell him to go there and check things out before you try to go in. Did you call the police yet?"

"No, I didn't know if maybe one of the boys forgot to close the door when they left home earlier. Marlin's leaving work now, so I'm waiting out here in the car for him to get here."

"Well, I don't want you to have to do that. Is anybody at Jerome's house? When I left for work a few minutes ago, there was a crowd of people over there. I bet somebody there might've seen something if somebody did go in your house."

"Oh no," Melissa quickly spoke up, "you must not have heard what happened to Jerome?"

"To Jerome? No." I hadn't heard any rumors about him over the past year and a half since court. Heck, I had no reason to be discussing him anyway since I was finally living in peace.

"Oh... Girl, Jerome's dead. He got killed early the other morning."

"What?" I could not believe what I was hearing.

"Yes, Girl. He got hit by a car when him and his girlfriend were riding on one of those back roads around the corner from our neighborhood...